Writing for the Workplace

Writing for the Workplace

Business Communication for Professionals

Janet Mizrahi

Writing for the Workplace: Business Communication for Professionals

First published in 2015 by
Business Expert Press, LLC
222 East 46th Street, New York, NY 10017
www.businessexpertpress.com

ISBN-13: 978-1-63157-232-6 (paperback)
ISBN-13: 978-1-63157-233-3 (e-book)

Business Expert Press Corporate Communication Collection

Collection ISSN: 2156-8162 (print)
Collection ISSN: 2156-8170 (electronic)

Cover and interior design by Exeter Premedia Services Private Ltd., Chennai, India

First edition: 2015

10 9 8 7 6 5 4 3 2 1

Printed in the United States of America.

Abstract

Employers consider communication one of the most critical skills for workers today. *Writing for the Workplace: Business Communication for Professionals* is an easy-to-follow guide that provides strategies for effective professional communication. Written to address the needs of both students entering the workforce and business professionals looking to improve their written communication, the book offers guides to compose typical workplace documents, from effective e-mails and convincing reports to winning presentations and engaging resumes. This concise book offers busy readers concrete strategies to improve their workplace writing.

Part I addresses writing in today's fast-paced business and professional contexts and discusses writing as a process, professional writing style, writing tools, characteristics of effective workplace communication, and basic document design. Part II is a more detailed exploration of common written genres in the workplace and discusses correspondence such as e-mail messages, letters, memos, and social media for specific workplace situations. Part III delves into short and long reports and business presentations, and Part IV is dedicated to employment communication. Each section includes many sample documents and examines organization, tone, and genre elements. A list of common writing errors to avoid, helpful checklists, and easily scannable text make the book accessible and readable.

Keywords

business communication, business presentations, business writing, e-mails, employment communication, negative news, persuasive writing, professional communication, professional writing, reports, routine news, workplace writing

Contents

Preface

For many, writing comes naturally. For others, it is a dreaded chore. Even if you enjoy writing, however, you may never have learned to write effective e-mails, memos, letters, or business reports. In many cases, the way you may have written in the past—using inflated language and long, rambling sentences to sound smart, or padding your work by repeating points to eke out a predetermined number of pages—is the exact opposite of the kind of writing valued in the professional world.

Many of us enter the workplace clueless about the right way to frame a request or compose a routine e-mail. We may wonder about issues such as how the document should look, what tone to adopt, or which organizational strategy to use. This book is designed to guide you through the steps to become a stronger, more effective writer in the world of work. Part I will focus on writing as a professional and cover topics such as the writing process, characteristics of professional writing, and the basics of document design. Part II will address correspondence. Part III will focus on reports and presentations. Part IV is devoted to employment communication. Appendix A contains explanations of common usage errors; Appendix B contains sample documents linked to specific chapters.

My hope is that this short guide will help you feel more confident as you write for every job you ever have.

Acknowledgments

I am lucky to have people in my life who have made me a better teacher and writer. Thanks to my colleagues at the University of California, Santa Barbara (UCSB): Dr. LeeAnne Kryder, my most ardent advocate and friend; Jeffrey Hanson, whose expertise and kindness never cease to amaze me; and Dr. Gina Genova, the best collaborator anyone could ask for. I would also like to thank Dr. Mary Ellen Guffey for always pushing me and for making me part of her team, and Dr. Dana Loewy, whose intelligent guidance and superb edits I so appreciate. And last but certainly not least, thanks to my husband, Perry Hambright, whose knowledge of graphics continues to make me look good.

PART I

Writing as a Professional

CHAPTER 1

Fundamentals of Professional Writing

Whether you are a student about to step into the world of work or a more seasoned employee with years of experience, you must be able to communicate effectively to advance your career. Employers consistently rank good communication skills—speaking with customers and colleagues, presenting information, and writing—in the top tier of desired skills for both new hires and current employees. The ability to concisely and accurately convey meaning to different people is a prerequisite in today's fast-paced world.

Writing like a professional—whether the document is printed or on the screen—is best taken on as a process, with careful attention paid to detail. This chapter will describe how to break down all writing tasks into a series of steps to streamline the process as well as describe the characteristics that all professional writing should embody.

Writing as a Process

Many people think that good writing flows out of the brain, into the fingers, and onto the page or screen. Nothing could be further from the truth. Professional writers know that writing, like any acquired skill, requires patience and persistence. Whatever we are composing—whether an e-mail message or a proposal for a new business—the key to writing well is to consider writing a process rather than a one shot deal. Your prose will be better and will take you less time to compose if you look at writing as a series of tasks. For those who suffer from writer's block or who shudder at the thought of writing, I can promise that if you break down writing into several component parts, the result will be better and you will feel less anxious.

The task of writing can be broken down to three separate steps, for which I've developed an acronym: **AWE**, short for assess, write, and edit.

These three steps should be completed for every piece of writing that will be seen by another person. The only writing that doesn't require this process is personal writing.

Step 1: Assess

Before you ever put your fingers on the keyboard or put pen to paper, begin by assessing the writing situation and define your **audience and purpose**. I advise making this step formal: Write down your answers.

Knowing the audience—your reader—is imperative for successful writing. Writers need to be very clear about the end user because the language and style we use depends upon who will read what we write. In essence, we have to psych out the reader to accomplish our writing goal. We cannot do that unless we analyze the reader accurately.

Define the characteristics of your reader as is shown in Table 1.1:

Begin the audience analysis portion of the first stage of the writing process (assessing) by completing an audience profile template, using the criteria mentioned in Table 1.1.

The next part of assessing the writing situation is defining your **purpose**. The reason or purpose for writing in the professional world falls into three basic categories: informing, persuading, or requesting. Informative writing is a large category that includes generalized information, instructions, notifications, warnings, or clarifications. Persuasive writing makes an impression, influences decisions, gains acceptance, sells, or recommends. Requests are written to gain information or rights and to stimulate action.

Unless you define the desired outcome of the written task, you cannot possibly achieve that task's objective. Are you writing an e-mail in response to a customer complaint? Are you using social media to generate traffic to a website selling nutritional supplements? You must be clear about what you want your words to accomplish before you write.

Sometimes you do not have all the information on hand that you need to write your document. Once you have defined for whom you are writing and what you want to accomplish, continue your analysis of the writing situation by gathering the information to produce the document. Sometimes that will entail conducting **research**. Sometimes you may just need to download information from your experience. Either way, have your information on hand *before* you begin to write. Nothing is

Table 1.1 Audience profile template

Audience characteristic	Rationale
Age	Writing for children differs from writing for adults or teens. Your tone, word choice, and medium may differ greatly depending on the age of the reader.
Gender	Writing for an all-male audience will differ from writing for an all-female audience. Likewise, if the audience is mixed, you may make different language choices than you do for a homogeneous group.
Language proficiency	The reader's knowledge of English will affect your word choice, sentence length, and other stylistic elements.
Education level	You may be writing for an audience with a 10th grade reading level or one comprised of college graduates. Each audience will have different expectations and needs, both of which you as the writer must be aware.
Attitude toward writer or organization	You must know if the audience is skeptical, frightened, pleased, or hostile toward you, the topic, or the organization. Anticipate your audience's reaction so you can write in a way that will support the document's purpose.
Knowledge of the topic	A document may be geared to people who are experts in a field or who know nothing about it. Even within an organization, several different audiences will exist. You may emphasize different aspects of a topic depending upon the readers' knowledge level.
Audience action	What do you want your audience to do after reading? Click a link for more information? Call to take advantage now? You must have a clear vision of your goal in communicating for your writing to be effective.

more frustrating than being on a deadline to compose a writing job and realizing that you do not have the information you need.

Once you have the information, **organize** it. For shorter pieces, think about the organizational structure you need to follow to attain your writing purpose. We will discuss these writing strategies in greater detail in Section 2. For longer pieces, begin by creating categories of information. From these sections, draft an **outline** with headings.

This assessing portion of the writing process will make the actual writing much easier. Why? It is always easier to begin writing if you have something on the page rather than nothing.

Step 2: Write

Enter the second step of the writing process—writing a draft—knowing that it is not the last step. A draft by definition is not final. Its purpose is to transfer the information you have gathered onto the page. For short documents such as routine e-mails, consider composing offline. (It's too tempting to write and hit send without carefully going over your draft!) Begin by including the information you've gathered, making sure you include each point. For longer documents, use your outline. Write section by section, point by point. If you have trouble with one section, move to another.

Your goal at this stage of the writing process for both short and longer documents is to put something down on paper (or the screen) that you will revise later. It's a waste of your valuable time to labor over any individual word or sentence as you write your draft; the word or sentence may be eliminated by the final version. If you cannot think of the precise word you need, leave a blank and return later to fill it in. If you are having difficulty wording a sentence smoothly, leave a bracketed space or perhaps type a few words as a reminder of the gist of what you want to say. The important point to remember is that a first draft is one of several stabs you'll take at this work.

If you write using information you have taken from other sources, avoid using someone else's words or ideas without attributing them. **Plagiarism** occurs when you use or closely imitate the ideas or language of another author without permission. Even if you paraphrase through rewording, you should still cite the source to avoid plagiarizing. With the abundance of material available to us with a few keystrokes, it's tempting to cut and paste and call it a day. But you leave yourself and your organization open to criminal liability for copyright infringement laws if you use words, images, or any other copyrighted material. Besides, you will never learn to express yourself if you use others' words.

Before you move to the next step, I advise printing your draft. But don't read it immediately. Let it marinate. It's too hard to edit our own copy immediately after we've written it. We need to let some time pass before we return to a draft so that we can be more objective when we edit.

Step 3: Edit

I saw a great T-shirt at a meeting for the Society for Technical Writers. On the front was the word *write* in bold type. Following that was line after line of the word *edit*. The final boldface word at the end of the last line was *publish*. Of course, the idea is that writing requires more editing than writing.

Editing is a multistepped process and begins by looking at the overall effectiveness of the piece. As you read your draft, return to your audience and purpose analysis and ask yourself if the content meets the needs of the audience while it accomplishes your purpose in writing. Does the document provide all the information readers will need to do what you want? Does it make sense? Is it well organized? If not, go back and make changes.

Once you are certain that the content is correct and complete, it's time for **paragraph and sentence level editing**. This is where you'll need a good style guide (see discussion of Writing Tools), unless you are one of the few who have perfect recall of all grammatical rules. Begin by examining the effectiveness of each paragraph. By definition, a paragraph is a group of sentences about one topic; the topic is generally stated in the first sentence of a paragraph and is called a topic sentence. Good paragraphs have **unity**, which means they stay on topic, so first check each paragraph for unity. Make sure your paragraphs aren't too long. Long paragraphs scare readers off.

Next check your paragraphs for **cohesion**, meaning that each sentence leads logically to the next. A common writing error is to jump from one idea to the next without providing a logical connection between those two ideas. Unless each idea expressed in a sentence logically segues to the next, your reader will not be able to follow. Writers link ideas several ways:

1. Using transitional words and phrases. Transitions are broken down into types: adding information, contrasting information, comparing information, illustrating a point, and showing time.
2. Using pronouns that refer back to a specific noun.
3. Repeating keywords to remind a reader of a central idea.

Table 1.2 illustrates the types of transitions writers use to compose cohesive sentences and paragraphs.

Table 1.2 Types of transitions

Type of transition	Words or phrases used
Additive—used to augment an idea	additionally, again, also, and, in addition, moreover, thus
Contrast—used to show how ideas differ	although, but, conversely, however, instead, on the other hand, yet
Comparison—used to link similar ideas	likewise, similarly
Time—used to show a sequence	after, finally, first, in the meantime, later, next, second, soon

Once all paragraphs are edited, examine each sentence. Now is the time to nitpick grammar and stylistic elements. Pay special attention to egregious errors such as:

1. Subject and verb agreement
2. Comma splices
3. Sentence fragments
4. Run-on sentences
5. Dangling modifiers

Find every pronoun to make sure it agrees with its antecedent and that the noun to which it refers is clear. Make sure you have written numbers in the correct way, using numerals and spelling out numbers appropriately. Stay in the same verb tense.

Also beware of dangling modifiers, phrases that confuse readers by saying something other than what is meant. They often appear in an introductory phrase at the beginning of a sentence but omit a word that would clarify meaning in the second part of the sentence. Look at the following sentence:

After finishing the copy, the website was difficult to understand.

The website did not finish the copy; therefore the meaning is obscure. Perhaps the sentence should have read:

After finishing the copy, the writer found that the website was difficult to understand.

As you edit, take some time to **read** your document **aloud** and make marks next to areas that require editing. This is the single best way to improve your writing. Professional writing should sound natural. If you find yourself stumbling as you read your copy, the chances are good that you have a problem; your ears will not allow you to pass over stylistic elements that your eye will just ignore. Listen for frequent repetition of the same word, for short, choppy sentences, and for sentences that begin with the same word or phrase. Make sure your sentences have variety in length, aiming for a good mix of short, medium, and longer sentences. Note whether you have started too many sentences with *there is, there are, this is*, or *it is*. Overuse of this wordy construction is a red alert for any professional writer to rewrite. Finally, make sure you have used words according to their actual definition, called the denotation. (Use the Avoiding Wordiness Checklist at the end of this chapter to help you edit for conciseness.)

The final element of the editing portion of the writing process is **proofreading**. Proofreading includes editing your copy for spelling, capitalization, punctuation, and typos. Begin by double-checking the correct spelling of names. Then make sure you've correctly used words that are commonly mistaken (i.e., affect and effect, complimentary and complementary). If you have included a phone number or a URL in the content, determine both are correct by phoning or checking the link.

A warning about using your word processor's spell check function: Spell check is far from fail proof. Just the omission of one letter (say the last *s* in *possess*) can change the word's meaning, and the program won't pick that up. *Posses* is a word (the plural of posse) but it isn't the word you meant to use. Additionally, a spellchecker won't find names spelled incorrectly or words not in its dictionary.

Proofreading for punctuation is critical. Proper use of commas makes a huge difference in a document's readability. Be especially on the lookout for inserting commas after introductory phrases and between two independent clauses joined by a coordinate conjunction. Likewise, tossing in a comma or semicolon haphazardly or omitting a comma or semicolon are common writing errors that affect readability. Both can affect flow and meaning. Consider how the comma alters these two sentences:

That, I'm afraid, has not been the case.
That I'm afraid has not been the case.

The first sentence refers to a previous statement and conveys the meaning that an earlier statement is untrue. The second means that the individual claims to be unafraid.

Capitalization is another part of the proofreading stage. Use your style guide to know when to capitalize nouns and titles and be consistent. Next examine the appearance of what you've written. Remember that copy must not only be well written; it must look attractive on the page or screen to maximize readability. You may find the Editing and Proofreading Checklist at the end of this chapter a helpful tool to guide you through this portion of the writing process.

You will find a list of common writing errors to avoid in Appendix A.

Professional Writing Characteristics

Writing for the world of work has certain characteristics that form the underpinning of anything you write, from an e-mail to your boss, to a resume for a new job, to a proposal for new business. Integrate the following elements into your work.

Accuracy

One of the best ways we can illustrate to our readers that we are professionals and experts is through accuracy. Inaccuracies show a carelessness that few professionals or organizations can afford in a competitive, global marketplace. Attention to accuracy is therefore paramount to professionals.

Active Voice

To enliven your prose, avoid using passive voice construction when you can. Passive voice makes the object of an action the subject of a sentence, as the following example illustrates:

Passive voice	*The e-mail was written by me.*
Active voice	*I wrote the website.*

However, if you wish to obscure the person committing an action, you *should* use passive voice. You do so by avoiding naming the actor, as is illustrated below:

Passive voice	*The students were given poor grades.*
Active voice	*The professor gave the students poor grades.*

If you have trouble identifying your own use of passive voice, you can adjust the Grammar Tools in Microsoft Word's Preferences, which when activated, will point out passive voice construction. If you are using passive voice purposefully because you want to sound objective, great. But if you have used passive voice unintentionally, change it.

Avoiding Gender, Racial, or Age Bias

English doesn't make biases easy to avoid. The best way to stay away from the he or she conundrum is to use the plural of a word. To avoid racial or age biases, beware of stereotypes when composing. Even if you feel the reference is complimentary, those to whom you refer may find that reference offensive.

Clarity

If a reader has to reread to understand anything you write, you have not done your job. Every sentence you write that another person will see should be easy to read. Clarity comes from using words the audience will recognize and using them correctly. Stay away from jargon or SAT-prep vocabulary. One way to check your work for clarity is to give your draft to someone who knows nothing about what you are writing. If that reader can understand the document, it is probably clear.

Conciseness

Busy professionals are impatient and expect brevity. No one wants to wade through wordy prose to get to a point. As mentioned earlier, the

Avoiding Wordiness Checklist at the end of this chapter contains some tips to make your writing more concise.

Conversational Prose with Smooth Flow

The rhythm of any prose needs to be conversational and natural. The best way to achieve good flow is to read your document aloud and keep amending until you are able to read without hesitation. Use simple, plain language in sentences that are not complex or convoluted. Make sure your punctuation does not impede your reader by adding unnecessary halts or by avoiding pauses that will aid understanding.

To make your prose more conversational, you can also use contractions when appropriate. Instead of *they will*, use *they'll*. You can also begin your sentences with *and* or *but*, which many English teachers taught as an inviolable rule. Sometimes beginning a sentence with a conjunction gives prose just the right rhythm to create that highly desired conversational tone.

Correctness

Poor grammar and words used incorrectly make both the writer and the organization appear ignorant and sloppy. To hone your grammatical skills, work with a grammar guide next to you. (The use of writing tools is discussed later in this chapter.) Consult the guide when you are unsure about any writing issue. Make use of your word processor's grammar and spell check, but do not rely on them solely. Another way to work on grammar issues is to create a *never again* table (see Table 1.3). This is a three-column table (see the following sample) that lists a grammatical error, the rule that governs the problem, and a mnemonic device to remember the solution. When you

Table 1.3 Never again table

Grammar problem	Rule	Mnemonic device
Its versus It's	It's **always** = it is	The dog bites its tail because it's plagued with fleas.
Effect versus affect	Effect = noun Affect = verb	Ibuprofen adversely affects my stomach, but the medicine's effect cures my headache.

keep a list of grammatical errors and refer to it as you compose, you will eventually learn to correct the problem. Keep adding and erasing errors until you no longer need to consult the chart.

Parallelism

Good writing often uses a device called parallelism, or parallel structure. Writers use parallelism instinctually because it appeals to our natural desire for symmetry. Parallelism matches nouns with nouns, verbs with verbs, and phrases with phrases: "For *faster* action, *less* stomach upset, and *more* for your money, use XX." Readers expect parallelism, especially in sets of two or three items, and in bulleted and enumerated lists. Using parallel phrasing correctly is key to writing in the workplace.

Positive Voice

Positive voice uses affirmative words to make a point. For example, instead of saying, "We are out of green T-shirts," we would emphasize the positive and say, "Order any size of our orange and gray T-shirts." Avoid downbeat words or words than can convey a negative connotation and rephrase in a positive way. Instead of, "No coupons will be honored after April 30," say, "Coupons will be honored through April 30."

Reliance on Strong Nouns and Verbs

Good writing uses nouns and verbs to do the heavy work and saves adverbs and adjectives for rare occasions. Instead of "Our brightly-colored, twinkling lights will be reminders of the happiest, most memorable times you and your family will ever enjoy," say, "Our dazzling lights will twinkle their way into your family's memories." Replace "Our auto policies are competitive," with "Our auto policies beat the competition's." Avoid using the most boring and overused verb in the English language: to be. Check for overuse of *is*, *are*, *were*, and *was* and see if you can eliminate them by using a stronger, more specific verb. We can't entirely avoid adverbs or adjectives or *to be*, but we can be mindful of how often we use them.

Sentence Variety

Sentence variety is linked to conversational prose and has two elements. The first is sentence beginnings. As you edit, look at the way your sentences begin. Do three in a row begin with *The*? Do two sentences within two paragraphs begin with *There are*? Avoid writing sentences that begin with the same word or phrase. The second way to attain sentence variety is to vary sentence length. Short, choppy sentences make prose annoyingly staccato. Natural-sounding prose combines short, medium, and longer sentences.

One way to check your sentence length is to look at how the periods line up. If you see a vertical or slanted line of periods, you need to alter some of the sentence lengths. This can be accomplished in several ways. Join two sentences whose content is closely linked by embedding the gist of one sentence into another. Combine two sentences with a coordinate conjunction to create a complex sentence. Or try an alternate sentence beginning such as an introductory phrase, which will add sentence variety.

Simple Words

Avoid jargon. Always, always, always choose the simpler, more recognizable word over the longer, more showy one. Instead of *rhinovirus* say *a cold*. Opt for *e-mail* over *electronic message*. In *utilize* versus *use*, *use* wins! (Also notice how the number of words your reader has to wade through goes down with simpler words.)

Shorter Paragraphs

Long paragraphs are appropriate for essays, but they have no place in professional documents. Big blocks of type scare readers away. The longest paragraph should be no more than six to eight lines. Always be aware of how a paragraph appears on a page (or a screen) and take pity on your audience—don't make your reader slog through dense prose.

Style: Formal versus Informal

Writers must wear different hats and adjust their writing style—sometimes called voice or tone—to the task at hand. In professional writing, we always aim for a natural style, as mentioned earlier. However, we must sometimes be even more specific about the style we choose.

Choosing to use an informal or formal writing style depends on the audience and the document's purpose. There is no clear-cut way to determine when to use each style; sometimes, an e-mail may require formality. Most of the time, however, e-mails are informal. To determine which style fits your needs, understand that informal writing allows the writer and reader to connect on a more personal level. It can convey warmth. Formal writing, on the other hand, produces the impression of objectivity and professionalism.

Some genres, however, have generally accepted styles. Use Table 1.4 to help guide you in choosing which style best suits your task.

Table 1.4 Formal and informal writing styles

	Formal style	Informal style
Types of documents	Letters Long reports Research Proposals	Most communication within the organization including e-mail, IM, memos, text messages Routine messages to outside audiences Informal reports
Characteristics	No personal pronouns (I, we) No contractions Objective voice or use of passive voice No figurative language or clichés No editorializing Limited use of adjectives No exclamation points Longer sentences Some technical language	Use of personal pronouns Use of contractions Shorter sentences, easily recognizable words Limited use of warm, inoffensive humor

Writing Tools

Just as a doctor wouldn't enter an examination room without a stethoscope or a carpenter wouldn't pull up to a job site without a hammer, no writer can be without the tools of the trade: a good dictionary, thesaurus, and style guide.

Many excellent writing reference books are on the market, both in electronic and print format. I use both. Although I often visit www.dictionary.com when I compose, I also rely on my hard copy dictionary. Dictionaries in book format allow us to browse, and sometimes the writer will happen upon a word or meaning, which doesn't happen when you use Dictionary.com. The same goes for the thesaurus. I find the thesaurus built into Microsoft Word to be very weak. As a writer, I need to make the most out of the bounteous English language. A hard cover thesaurus is worth its weight in gold as far as I'm concerned. I use *Roget's 21st Century Thesaurus* edited by Barbara Ann Kipfer, PhD. I particularly like that it's organized like a dictionary.

Many good style guides are likewise available. For a grammar guide, I use Diana Hacker's *A Writer's Reference*, 7th edition, but many excellent grammar reference books are available.

Many good grammar websites can also be useful. The Grammar Book (http://www.grammarbook.com/) and the Purdue Online Writing Lab (https://owl.english.purdue.edu/) are handy and reliable websites to look up any grammar issues you may have.

The important thing to remember is to keep your tools nearby as you compose. The more you use these references, the less you'll need them. You will internalize the rules of writing as you use them.

Conclusion

Writing well on the job is key to career success. By breaking down writing into stages called the writing process, your end product is more likely to accomplish its ultimate purpose. When composing on the job, effective writers integrate many elements that will distinguish their work as professional, well-edited, and clear. Whether you choose hard copy or digital, use writing tools including a dictionary, thesaurus, and grammar guide to create professional documents. Doing so will help you excel in the workplace.

Avoiding Wordiness Checklist

Wordy phrase and example	Solution	✓
Avoid beginning a sentence with *There are* or *It is*. *There are four points that should be considered.* *It is clear that cashmere is warmer.*	Begin sentences with the true subject. *Consider these four points* or *Four points should be considered.* *Cashmere is clearly warmer.*	
Avoid beginning sentences with *That* or *This*. *Choosing teams should be done carefully. This is because a good mix will generate better results.*	Connect to previous sentence. *Choosing teams should be done carefully because a good mix will generate better results.*	
Use *active voice* rather than passive. *Rain forests are being destroyed by uncontrolled logging.*	Passive voice depletes prose of vitality and can almost always be rewritten in active voice. *Uncontrolled logging is destroying rain forests.*	
Omit *that* or *which* whenever possible. *The water heater that you install will last 15–20 years.*	Unless that or which is required for clarity, omit it. *The water heater you install will last 15–20 years.*	
Avoid prepositional phrase modifiers. *The committee of financial leaders meets every Tuesday.*	Replace with one-word modifiers. *The financial leaders committee meets every Tuesday.*	
Avoid *be* verbs. *New Orleans is one of the most vibrant cities in the United States.*	Replace with a strong verb. *New Orleans vibrates with activity like no other U.S. city.*	
Tighten closely related sentences of explanation. *When hanging wallpaper, three factors need to be considered. The factors are X, X, and X.*	Join closely related sentences of explanation with a colon to avoid repetitions. *When hanging wallpaper, consider three factors: X, X, and X.*	
Tighten closely related sentences. *MRIs are used to diagnose many ailments. MRIs create an image of organs and soft tissues to diagnose.*	Omit repetitious phrasing in second sentence. *MRIs diagnose many ailments by creating images of organs and soft tissues.*	

(*Continued*)

Avoiding Wordiness Checklist (*Continued*)

Wordy phrase and example	Solution	✓
Tighten verb phrases with auxiliary + ing verbs *Management was holding a staff meeting.*	Replace is/are/was/were/have + verb with a one-word verb. *Management held a staff meeting.*	
Avoid using *there is/are* within a sentence. *When creating a mail list, there are many pitfalls.*	Find an active verb to replace *there is/are.* *When creating a mail list, many pitfalls exist.*	
Remove redundancies. *An anonymous stranger may be dangerous.*	Know the true meaning of a word. *Strangers may be dangerous.*	

Editing and Proofreading Checklist

Check your draft for the following	✓
Document content is tailored to meet the needs of the audience and attains writing purpose	
Copy is edited for conciseness	
Body paragraphs have unity and cohesion and are shortened for visual appeal	
Transitions in and between paragraphs adequately link ideas	
Grammar is correct	
Punctuation is used correctly	
Copy has good rhythm and flow; uses a natural and conversational tone	
Sentences show variety in beginning and length	
Names are spelled correctly; phone numbers and URLs are accurate	
Words are used correctly	
Capitalization is consistent and adheres to specific stylebook guidelines	
Document adheres to specific genre formatting guidelines	
Document shows professionalism	

CHAPTER 2

Basics of Document Design

One of the most important elements of workplace writing is a document's appearance. Writing in professional contexts requires as much attention to the way a document appears on the page or the screen as its content. The reason is that as writers, we must make the task of reading easy for our audience. If you have ever waded through dense pages of text with long paragraphs or tried to follow a single line of type that goes across an 18-inch computer screen, you know that reading can become tedious if good design is not factored into what your eyes must look at.

In this chapter, we'll cover the basics of document design for print and screen. We will discuss the conventions of document design as they pertain to specific genres in the remaining chapters.

Print Document Design

Writing for a printed page differs from writing for a screen not just in the words we write but in the way the words look on the page. This is called **page layout**. You are probably aware of certain elements of page layout without knowing it. For example, use of columns and choice of landscape or portrait view are part of page layout.

When composing a document that will be printed, first consider page size. Is your document for standard sized paper (8.5 × 11 in.) or smaller? If you are creating a trifold brochure, for example, you will be laying out the words very differently than if you are writing a report. In both cases, however, consider the z pattern. The z pattern (see Figure 2.1) is the way readers of English approach a page. Our eye begins at the top left of the page and scans to the right, going back and forth, left to right, until we reach the bottom. This pattern is significant because words or images that fall along the z hold the eye's attention more than the areas surrounding

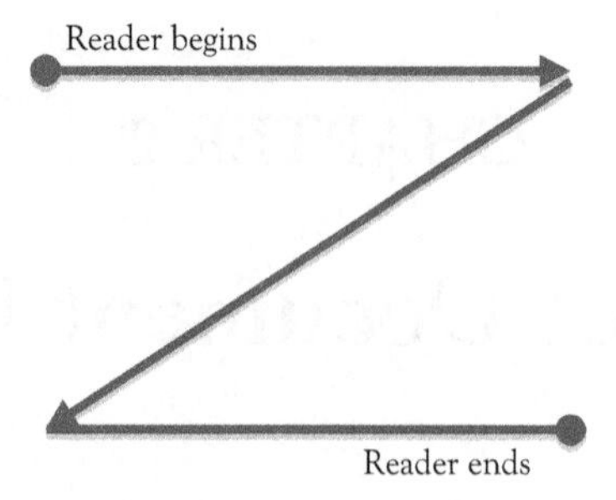

Figure 2.1 Z pattern of reading

the z. Savvy writers will put words and images they want the reader to focus on along this path.

Elements of Page Layout

Each page contains design elements you will want to consider as follows.

Color

Although black is always the preferred color for body type, some color can add visual interest to print pages. Color can be used for document headings, in charts and graphs, or as ways to highlight information. Avoid using bright colors for type and understand that the way a color appears on the screen will likely differ from its reproduction on the printed page. Also remember that you will need a color printer for your color scheme to show!

Graphical Elements

Adding graphical elements to your documents such as boldface, bullets, enumeration, italics, or underlining serve varied functions. **Boldface** calls attention to words and phrases. It is commonly used for headings and sparingly used to highlight words or phrases. **Bulleted points** are used to list items and to attract the reader's eye. Bulleted points break up text, too. **Enumeration** (listing items 1., 2., 3., etc.) is used to indicate a series in order. *Italics* are used for emphasis, to indicate a word in a different language, for proper names, and for titles. **Underlining** can indicate a title or emphasis.

A quick word on the use of CAPS. Beware that the reader will interpret type in all caps as a scream. The only time I use all caps is in a context in which I must conform to a text-only design. In that case, I use caps for headings. I never use all caps and boldface, however. It is not only redundant but also truly a signal for translating the words into a scream.

No graphical elements should be overused, and writers should avoid including too many on any one page. Doing so clutters the page and ends up having the opposite effect from what was intended.

Headings and Subheadings

Headings name categories of information. They summarize the content that follows and are organized by levels: first level heading, second level heading, and so forth. Headings can be viewed as the points of an outline, and their use is a primary way writers organize content. For the reader, headings serve as graphic markers that signal a new topic. They help the reader easily focus on specific areas of interest. Headings break up text, making material more visually attractive and easier on the eye.

Subheadings are mini-headings, or subsections of a heading. They, too, break up long text and enhance visual appeal.

In a print document, headings are indicated by use of a graphical device such as centering, boldface, or caps. Headings often use a contrasting type font. For example, if the body of a report were Times New Roman, you might want to use Arial for headings.

Header and Footer

Using a header and footer is a way to unify a document. Headers and footers also provide a location of page numbers or add graphic design features such as a company logo.

Margins

Most business documents have page margins all around of 1 to 1.5 in. Page margins are important because they create white space to make a page look uncluttered. Another aspect of margins is **justification**. Word processing programs give you four options for your margins: left justified with a ragged right edge, centered, right justified with ragged left, and fully justified. Table 2.1 illustrates the types of margin justification and when each should be used.

Table 2.1 Type justification

Type justification	Functionality
This margin is left justified, ragged right type. This margin is left justified, ragged right. This margin is left justified, ragged right.	Notice how the left margin forms a straight line, while the right edge is jagged. This is considered the easiest alignment to read and should be used in nearly every writing situation.
This is centered type. This is centered type. This is centered	Centered type is inappropriate for most reading tasks but is a good choice for headings, such as the headings in this table.
This is right justified type with a ragged left margin this is right justified type with a ragged left margin	Readers' eyes would quickly tire if having to readjust to locate the beginning of each line of type. Use right justified type to align short phrases only.
This line is considered fully justified. This line is considered fully justified. This line is considered fully justified. This line is considered fully justified.	Notice the awkward spaces between the words when using fully justified text. This occurs because the word processor does not hyphenate words so it has to create spaces to fit the type into a rectangle. Those spaces slow down reading. When full justification is needed for particular documents, you will need to use your own appropriate word hyphenations to reduce the space gaps that otherwise occur.

Paragraph Length

In college papers, it is not unusual for a paragraph to take up an entire typed page. However, that this is unacceptable in all business documents. To aid our readers, business writers limit paragraph length to no more than eight lines (not eight sentences.) This is a rule of thumb that should be taken very seriously. Long, dense paragraphs scare readers away.

Spacing

Again, in college, papers are usually double spaced and new paragraphs are indented. However, in business documents, single spacing is the norm; new paragraphs are signaled by adding an extra space. Because the extra space is clearly a marker of a new paragraph, it would be redundant and unnecessary to also use a tab.

Typeface

Type fonts are divided into two basic families: *serif* and *sans serif.* Serif fonts such as Times, Garamond, or Palatino have feet and tails under the letters that form a line to help the eye track the words and sentences, which is why graphic artists choose serif fonts for long documents such as books. Serif fonts have an old fashioned feel. For business documents that will be printed, using a serif font will help your reader move through the content faster.

Sans serif fonts like Helvetica, Arial, and Verdana have a cleaner, simple line that translates better to the pixel-based display on screens.

Look at the following example to examine the difference between font families:

This is 12-point Garamond, a serif font.

This is 12-point Arial, a sans serif font.

Notice the difference in the two 12-point fonts. Both are 12-point, but Arial appears much larger than Garamond. When you choose your font, you will want to take into consideration how large or small it appears on the page.

White Space

Space on a page without any visual or type is called white space. White space breaks up text and frames the words on the page. It also helps balance a page. It is helpful to view your page in the *preview* function of the word processing tool you use to see how the white space is arranged on the page. This is an excellent way to adjust pages that are off balance or too densely packed with words.

Word Processing Defaults and Templates

Word processing is no doubt a blessing for everyone who has to write. It's hard to imagine not being able to instantly rearrange paragraphs or delete sentences. However, when using word processing, it's a good idea to keep its limitations in mind.

One point to examine is your application's default document design. You will find the newer default versions of Microsoft Word documents use 1.10 or 1.15 line spacing instead of 1.0, as is the norm. They also include sans serif fonts. These elements are easy enough to alter, but be aware that *you* must manipulate the default.

Word processing templates are a mixed blessing. Sometimes learning how to alter the preformatted document elements takes more time than creating your own. Using easily recognizable templates can make a writer appear lazy or unoriginal. In addition, I find that many templates ignore the basics of good design. On the other hand, Word's new newsletter and brochure templates make creating these documents easier than ever. Word also allows anyone to insert professional looking charts and other graphics into documents. In all cases, it's a good idea to be aware of the plusses and minuses of using defaults and templates.

Design Considerations for Digital Formats

Writing for the screen differs measurably from writing for a printed page. If you are writing anything from an e-mail you know will be read on a screen to a report saved as a PDF that the reader can print or read on the screen, you will need to understand the unique situation of composing for the screen.

The first thing to consider is that reading on a screen slows readers down. In fact, studies show that it takes readers 25 percent longer to read something on the screen than on paper.[1] The cause is likely due to screen resolution, despite the headway new electronic devices have made in this regard.

Another consideration is that people reading on screens scan and scroll. They tend to not read in a linear fashion (starting at the beginning and going to the end) and instead jump from heading to heading or section to section. For this reason, we must be aware of creating scannable text. Certain techniques make text more scannable. These include writing paragraphs of six lines maximum and using headings and bulleted points.

The following design elements affect writing for the screen.

Color: Writers have much freedom in color choice when writing words that readers will read on a screen. However, the best color for readability remains black type on white background. Bright colors like fuchsia or light colors such as yellow will be very hard for readers to decipher, even in headings. Do, however, use color selectively for your page design in reports designed to be read on the screen or documents such as resumes.

Font style and size: Because sans serif fonts are crisper, many people consider them easier to read on the screen. Indeed, many copy-heavy websites such as newspapers and magazines use serif fonts for their print editions and sans serif fonts for the online versions. However, some designers continue to use serif fonts for the screen. If you choose to do so, make sure the font is large enough for your intended reader and the spacing is adjusted.

It is also important to remember that the way you design your document may be affected by the end user's device and its settings. Unless you are providing a PDF, the way you design a document to be read on an electronic device may not be the way the receiver sees it.

Graphical elements: Much of the advice related to using graphical elements in print also applies to their use in electronic documents. But because we know readers have less patience when reading on the screen, devices to break up text and highlight important ideas, words, or phrases are even more important. Note that boldface can indicate a link, so when using it, make sure your readers will not be confused.

Headings: Headings in print and electronic documents serve the same function, but they are even more important for reading on the screen than reading on the page. The reason is that people tend to skip when reading on the screen. Headings, therefore, help readers find information quickly and make text more scannable.

Line length and spacing: Because screen reading is more taxing, keep lines on the short side, no more than 70 characters. Consider using two columns for reports that will be read on the screen.

Paragraph length: When writing for the screen, keep paragraphs short—about six lines—to avoid dense blocks of text.

White space: Lack of visual clutter will make any document more appealing for the reader. White space helps readers focus on words

Conclusion

Taking the time to consider how our words look on a page or a screen is imperative for writing in the workplace. Our job, after all, is to make the task of reading less of a chore. Considerations of type font, spacing, page layout, and graphical elements are as important to writing as are well-drafted sentences and paragraphs. A well designed document will make your writing more effective.

PART II

Correspondence

CHAPTER 3

Routine and Positive Messages

Much communication in the professional world will entail delivering routine messages such as requests for information or action, replies to customers, and explanations of policies or procedures. Goodwill messages—used to build relationships and extend warmth—are also a common type of routine message.

Routine messages are considered positive in situations when the reader will be pleased, interested, or feel neutral about the message. For example, if you were writing to a customer to confirm delivery of an order, the recipient would likely be pleased or at the very least feel neutral about the message. Similarly, if you were writing to congratulate a colleague about a promotion, the reader's reaction would be to feel pleased. The audience's expected response to any message dictates how that message is written. Positive messages are organized using a **direct approach**, which is constructed using three elements:

1. Opening stating the main purpose, subject, or idea
2. Body containing relevant details explaining the subject
3. Ending with a polite request, summary, or goodwill thought

We will discuss how this organizational strategy manifests itself in our discussion of specific genres later in this chapter.

The way you relay a positive or routine message—in other words, the type of media you select to transmit the message—depends on several factors. In some situations, your company may dictate communication protocol, in which case you must adhere to those guidelines. However, other times you may need to choose from the various types of media: e-mail, letter, memo, phone, or text message. Your choice will depend upon your audience, the level of formality the situation calls for, and your purpose in writing.

Use Table 3.1 to help you decide which media (also referred to as a *channel*) to choose for routine messages.

Table 3.1 Media communication channels

Media type	When to use
E-mail	For routine communication 24/7 that may not require immediate attention; used between coworkers in an organization and to outside stakeholders
Instant messaging	To receive immediate feedback from a coworker who is also online; also used in customer and vendor chats
Letter	For formal written documentation, especially with individuals outside of the organization
Memo	To present information, policies, procedures within an organization; to present short reports to external organizations
Text messaging	To leave short messages that may or may not be seen immediately by coworkers; also for some marketing messages to customers
Phone-direct conversation	For immediate feedback; to connect personally; in lieu of face-to-face meeting
Voice-mail message	To leave routine or important information (not highly sensitive in nature)

Whichever channel you use, remember that all professional communication must adhere to the message characteristics we discussed in Chapter 2.

Writing Routine Messages

Each of the previously listed media has specific characteristics. Here we will discuss the elements of most widely used written genres for routine and positive messages; sample documents of each genre appear in Appendix B.

E-mail

As a genre, e-mail is entrenched in the modern workplace. A recent survey found that workers look at their inboxes an average of 74 times a day.[1] Although text messages and video chats have replaced some e-mail, it is still an integral part of writing for work and critical for today's workforce.

In general, e-mail is used to exchange information with clients and colleagues any time of the day or night.[2] While that makes e-mail convenient for both reader and writer, it also means your message may not be read or responded to immediately. Therefore, e-mail should not be used for urgent issues. E-mail is also used when several or many people must view the same message.

Some say e-mail is most appropriate for short messages that require a response to an inquiry or ask for information.[3] However, it is not uncommon to see longer e-mails that deal with more complex issues. Likewise, e-mails often act as replacements for traditional letters or memos.

All e-mails contain basic elements you should incorporate into short, long, formal, or informal messages, as outlined in the following discussion.

Subject Line

An e-mail's subject line accurately and succinctly reflects the message's content. Working people are busy and their e-mail inboxes are packed with dozens or even hundreds of messages to sift through. Writing subject lines with specific wording that clearly identifies the topic will help your reader. Notice how the following vague subject line leaves the reader wondering, while the specific subject line leaves little to the imagination.

Vague subject line	New Policy
Specific subject line	New Parking Policy Effective June 1

When writing your subject line, avoid inflated or emotional appeals such as *Urgent* or *Critical Situation*. (If a situation is truly critical, you should probably phone the individual instead of sending an e-mail!) Also be aware of ethical choices when writing a subject line and don't make claims that are misleading or untrue. While it may be tempting to lure a reader into an e-mail by using a catchy subject line like *Free Subscription!* unless you are actually offering a free subscription, you are misleading readers, who will not appreciate being lured into a disingenuous e-mail that wastes their valuable time.

Greeting and Salutation

A greeting at the beginning of an e-mail is a visual cue that shows the recipient where to start reading. The type of greeting or salutation in an e-mail depends on the recipient and the level of formality required by the situation. Writing to an outside audience—those not in your organization—is usually a more formal situation, so use a person's title (Mr., Ms., Mrs., Dr., Prof.) until that individual replies using a first name. Once you are on a first name basis, you can tone down the level of formality and write "Dear Brad." You can also wrap the salutation into the first line of your e-mail as follows:

Thanks, Brad, for the information about the geothermic survey.

For less formal situations, use one of the following salutations:

Hi, Brad,
Hello, Brad,
Brad,
Good morning, Brad,

If a discussion thread—a series of e-mails on the same topic—is ongoing, you may find that a greeting becomes unnecessary. This is a common practice, but only after the thread of the conversation has gone on for several formal e-mails.

Finally, addressing a group differs from addressing individuals. If sending an e-mail blast to a list of customers, for example, you may want to choose a greeting such as "Dear Valued Customer." If sending an e-mail to a committee, it is appropriate to begin the correspondence with the committee's name, as noted in the following.

Dear Land Assessment Committee:

Avoid using the generic "To Whom It May Concern." Use of this greeting in an e-mail shows you haven't done your homework.[4] If an e-mail is replacing a traditional letter, use a standard letter salutation,[5] which we will discuss later in this chapter.

Opening

The first paragraph of e-mails delivering routine news or information should contain an expanded explanation of the topic mentioned in the subject line. For example, the opening for the e-mail about the new parking policy subject line we discussed earlier would begin by frontloading the first paragraph and elaborating on the subject.

Direct opening: A new policy giving preferred parking to carpools will take effect on Monday, June 1, 2016.

Restating the purpose of the e-mail in the first paragraph helps busy readers who may have skipped the subject line or who want to know exactly what they are reading about. Avoid indirect first paragraphs such as the following one, which unnecessarily take up your readers' time.

Wordy indirect opening: The committee on sustainable business practices has been working on policies to improve our company's green profile and has decided to institute a new plan giving carpools preferred parking spots effective June 1, 2016.

Body

The body of your e-mail contains the details required to fully understand the topic stated in both the subject line and opening. It should be written in short paragraphs of no more than six to eight lines and no more than 60 to 70 characters across (a character is a letter, punctuation, or a space.) In the body of the e-mail, use graphical markers, as we discussed in Chapter 2. Headings, white space, and bulleted or enumerated points break up text and make reading both short and long e-mails easier.

To avoid confusion, restrict each e-mail to one topic. Though it may seem counterintuitive, sending several consecutive e-mails to the same person, each covering one topic, will be more effective than trying to deal with too much in one e-mail for several reasons. First, many people do not read carefully and only focus on the beginning of the e-mail, scanning the rest. Second, receiving several e-mails with different subject lines allows your reader to pick which e-mail to respond to first. Finally, individually labeled e-mails, identified by specific subject lines, help the sender, too. If you have sent one person several e-mails on different topics, you will be happy to receive a reply to each item requiring your eyes rather than having to wade through one dense, long response.

Closing

A final paragraph, statement, or phrase that closes the e-mail helps readers understand what to do next or tells them that they have reached the end of the correspondence. End routine news by using one of these options:

- **Action information, dates, deadlines:** When you want readers to take an action, provide the information they need to do so. Assign an end date and time.
- **Summary of message:** In longer messages, you may want to recap the main points covered in the message.
- **Polite closing thought:** Express gratitude or encourage feedback, but avoid clichés such as "Please do not hesitate to call for further information."[6]

A closing helps avoid an abrupt ending to your e-mail and therefore sounding curt. Short closings such as *See you next week*, *All the best*, and *Warm regards* are less formal and are perfect for e-mails to coworkers or those with whom you have developed a cordial work relationship.

Signature Block

Always include your name at the end of any e-mail. Because e-mails are not written on letterhead, a signature block is used to provide contact information. E-mail applications contain options for using several different signature blocks. Formal e-mails—those going to outside vendors or customers or from an organizational leader to the staff—should contain complete contact information as is illustrated here.

Full Name and Title	Caroline Johnson, Design Manager
Organization Department	Creative Services
Organization Name	Mentor, Inc.
Mailing Address	3366 Broad Street, Portland, OR 97205
Phone/Fax	Phone: 503-877-9000 ext. 27/ Fax: 503-977-9300
Web Address	www.mentor.com

Less formal e-mails may contain modified signature blocks with less information or the addition of an extra line with the writer's first name, as shown in the following.

Best,

Carrie

Caroline Johnson, Design Manager

Creative Services

Tone

Because e-mail doesn't allow the reader to see body language or facial cues, hitting the right tone can be difficult. You may send an e-mail you consider to the point and concise, but your reader may consider it abrupt or terse. Likewise, you may insert a humorous tidbit that your reader finds silly or even offensive.

The best way to avoid being misunderstood is to be polite.[7] Reread your e-mail before you send it. If it sounds too blunt, add a *please* or *thank you* or acknowledge the individual on a personal level. Never use sarcasm, and be wary of humor. Peoples' definitions of what is funny differ greatly.

Another point: Do not use emoticons such as emojis in professional e-mails. If you need a facial expression to soften or add meaning to your words, your words are not properly chosen.

Document Design

To make your e-mails readable, follow these formatting guidelines.

- Limit length of lines to 60 to 70 characters
- Keep paragraph length to six to eight lines maximum
- Use left justified, ragged right margins
- Use single spacing for paragraphs, double spacing between paragraphs
- Employ graphical devices such as headings, white space, or bullets or enumeration as appropriate
- Include signature block

Short e-mails (up to one screen) may not require headings. However, the longer the e-mail, the more important it is to break up the text into clearly identifiable sections marked by well written headings.

E-mail Etiquette and Best Practices

A major complaint among people in the workforce is that e-mail clogs their inboxes and drains their time. One study found that the average employee in a corporation will spend more than one-fourth of each day dedicated to sending and reading e-mail and will receive more than 115 messages.[8] To help your e-mails gain your reader's attention, be aware of these best practices, sometimes called *netiquette*, for e-mail use (Table 3.2).

See Appendix B for an example of a routine news e-mail.

Letters

Letters are the preferred channel for documents that require a written record, especially when communicating with associations, the government, and customers. Print letters are also used in resignations and for recommendations. The benefit of a printed letter with a handwritten signature is that it conveys authority, formality, respect, and importance. Letters also stand out among the sea of e-mails most people receive daily.

When writing a letter whose purpose is to provide routine information or news or to request without using persuasion, use the direct approach outlined earlier. Whether you include a subject line or not, begin routine newsletters with a direct statement of the letter's purpose, as is shown in the following:

> It is with great pleasure that I write this recommendation for Kirsten Chen, with whom I had the pleasure of working for three years.
> We would be delighted to give your seventh grade students a tour of our newspaper's facilities on Thursday, July 17, as you requested.

Letters contain the following mandatory elements.

Letterhead

All letters should be written on letterhead stationery that includes the full address and contact information of the organization or the individual.

Table 3.2 E-mail best practices or netiquette

Limit e-mails to one topic.
Send e-mail only to those who must receive the information; use *cc* and *reply all* sparingly to reduce e-mail overload.
Use *bcc* (blind carbon copy) to send mass mailings so all e-mail addresses are not visible to the entire list of recipients; do not use *bcc* to send sensitive information.
Always include a clear subject line; change subject line when a discussion thread switches topic.
Never send an e-mail when angry (called *flaming*).
Avoid forwarding jokes, spam, or off-color remarks when using company devices.
Use a professional sounding e-mail address.
Be concise and get to the point quickly.
Hit the right level of formality. If you use a person's first name in person, use the first name in an e-mail. If you do not know a person, begin by using a title (*Hello, Ms. Chen*).
Never send an e-mail asking for information that has already been provided. It makes you look lazy or inattentive to detail.
Employ white space, headings, bullets, and short paragraphs to enhance readability.
Reply to e-mails within 24 hours, even if just to say you've received the message and will deal with it at a later date.
Edit carefully. Typos, misspellings, and grammatical errors undermine your credibility. Spell out rather than using abbreviations.
Mention attached documents in the body of the e-mail and make sure you have actually attached them.

Most organizations will have letterhead in both hard copy and electronic versions.

Date

The date the letter is being written should use no abbreviations (i.e., January 16, 2015, *not* Jan. 16, 2015.) Ordinals are *never* used in the date (1st, 2nd, 3rd, 24th, etc.).

Inside Address

The inside address contains the name and address of the person receiving the letter. The name should be preceded by a title (Mr., Ms., etc.). In today's workplace, it is common to refer to a woman as *Ms.* unless she has shown a preference to be labeled *Miss* or *Mrs.* Use professional titles (Dr. Professor, Senator) over generic titles. If sending a letter to someone in an organization, include the person's title under the name, followed by the name of the organization and its address:

Ms. Jeanine Bauer
Compliance Manager
Tri County Area Governments
232 South El Sueño Road
Santa Teresa, CA 93115

Salutation

Letters call for a formal salutation followed by a colon. If addressing a letter to an individual, write:

Dear Ms. Bauer:

If addressing two people, use:

Dear Ms. Bauer and Mr. Gresham:

When addressing a group, use a collective name such as *Committee, Members, Customers*:

Dear Hiring Committee:
Dear Valued Members:
Dear Loyal Customers:

Only include first and last name in a salutation if sending a letter to someone you do not know and the name is of ambiguous gender, such as *Pat Saunders* or *Chris Terlikian.*

Subject Line

Although not essential, some people add an informative subject line that foretells the letter's purpose and key facts,[9] such as this:

Subject: Student Tour of Daily News Facilities on July 17

Body

The message of the letter is considered the body. It should conform to the rules of effective professional communication that we've previously discussed: use of short paragraphs, bullets, headings (if appropriate), and white space to make a letter attractive and easy to read.

Complimentary Closing

The most traditional way to sign off a letter is with a complimentary closing such as *Sincerely* or *Cordially* followed by a comma. Use of *Thank you*, or *Best wishes*, also followed by a comma, may be used for less formal letters.

Signature Block

The sender's signature block follows the complimentary close. Allow three to four spaces for the handwritten signature, and type the sender's full name and title. Sign the full name (first and last) for formal letters, and the first name only for less formal letters. Do not include the address of the organization; doing so on letterhead would be redundant.

End Notes

Sometimes a business letter requires a notation, the last element on the page that comes two lines after the signature block. These include reference initials, enclosures, or copy notices. Reference initials are the typist's initials after the sender's. For example, say Jorge M. Marquez is sending the letter but his assistant, Leslie Adler, typed it. The reference initials would be: JMM:la or JMM/la

Whenever a letter contains something besides the letter, notify the reader with the notation *Enclosure* or *Enc*. If more than one enclosure is contained, the notation should indicate so: Enclosure (3).

If anyone else is receiving a copy of a letter, indicate that with the notation *c: John Doe.*

Letter Document Design

Some organizations have their own guidelines for letter design, which you must follow. Otherwise, the most common style for letters is the *block style*. Block style conforms to the following parameters:

1. Left align, ragged right
2. No paragraph tabs
3. Single spacing
4. Double spacing between paragraphs; do not indent

Other letter designs are modified block, in which the date, complimentary closing, and signature block are aligned about midway across the page. Whichever design you are using, always check the appearance of your letter in the preview mode of your word processing program. A letter should not be crammed into the top of the page; it should look balanced. If your letter is short, increase your margins and use a slightly larger font size. To help balance on the page, add white space above and below the date.

Your letter will have to go inside an envelope. Most word processing applications have an envelope function that allows you to type the return address (unnecessary if using a company envelope with preprinted return address). Never send a typed letter in a handwritten or printed envelope. If your letter is handwritten, however, a nearly handwritten envelope is acceptable. See Appendix B for an example of a letter.

Memos

Memos (or memoranda) are documents written within organizations, although they are sometimes used as a format for short reports sent to a recipient outside of the organization. They can be as short as one page or much longer and are used in situations that require a permanent or formal record. Types of memos include short reports, proposals, or other informational correspondence. Sometimes memos are printed; other times, they are sent as an attachment to an e-mail.

The writing strategy for routine memos is the same as that used in routine e-mails and letters. Begin with the purpose of the memo; use the body paragraphs to provide any details or explanations to support the main point; end with a forward looking closing that either summarizes the message (*We are certain that these new procedures will make our workplace safer and more comfortable*), asks for an action with an end date (*Please turn in your expense reports on the first working day of each month beginning in February*), or offers a polite, concluding thought (*I am looking forward to completing the project and for your feedback on our work to date*).

Memo Document Design

Memos are generally written on stationery with the organization's name on top. Full letterhead is unnecessary when the memo is going to an internal audience. Under the company name, the word Memo or Memorandum is centered. On the left margin, use the guidewords **Date:**, **To:**, **From:**, **Subject:**. Be sure to use the tab to align the information following the guidewords, as is illustrated in the sample memo in Appendix B. Skip three lines and then begin the memo. Use graphical devices such as headings, bulleted or enumerated points, and white space to break up text and to guide your reader. If a memo is longer than one page, number the pages. And of course, memos do not need to be signed, since the sender's name appears in the guidewords. However, you may write in your initials next to your name in the *From* line. See Appendix B for an example of a typical memo.

Text Messaging

The popularity of text messaging with smart phones has no doubt impacted every aspect of our lives, including the workplace. Today text messages have replaced some phone calls and e-mails for transmitting short messages in both large and small organizations.

Like e-mail, text messages should be used to transmit nonsensitive information. For example, it is perfectly acceptable to use a text message to notify a customer that an order has arrived.

If you are texting for work-related reasons, always follow company policies. If none have been established, ask your supervisor about the types of situations in which texting would be acceptable. Note that while it is common for texting between friends to use shorthand, emoticons, abbreviations, and lack of attention to grammar, such practices have *no* place on the job. Doing so shows a lack of professionalism that will not earn you respect.

Keep in mind the following points when texting for work.

- Never text sensitive or confidential material
- Keep text messages brief
- Use proper grammar and spelling
- Avoid texting while speaking to someone
- Identify yourself if texting someone you don't know

Types of Routine Messages

Various situations that arise in work situations call for specific types of routine messages. The choice of how these messages is delivered—whether via e-mail, letter, memo, or text—depends on the organization and situation. Consider the following explanations of the types of routine messages you may encounter in the workplace and details about how they are composed. Examples of these messages may be found in Appendix B.

Requests and Responses

Making and responding to requests comprise a good deal of the types of business messages you will be called upon to write. These types of routine messages are straightforward and call for the direct strategy. When writing routine requests, follow the following formula:

1. State the request directly in a polite, undemanding tone.
2. Provide details that explain the request, asking questions if necessary. Be sure you include all the information the reader will need to be able to respond adequately to your request. Whenever possible, add reader benefits (*Completing the form will allow us to process your order quickly*) to add the likelihood of a response.
3. End with a request for a specific action and show appreciation.

Replies or responses to requests should also use the direct strategy:

1. Respond directly to the inquiry in the opening.
2. Answer all questions in the body.
3. Encourage a positive response, if appropriate, or end with a polite goodwill statement.

See Appendix B for an example of a direct request and a direct request response.

Instructions

If you have ever put together a piece of furniture or electronic equipment using instructions, you know that clear, easy-to-understand instructions are rare. Writing instructions requires that you fully understand the steps or procedure and use language the reader will readily grasp.

When writing routine correspondence that contains instructions, use the direct strategy and follow these tips:

- Break down each task into a separate, numbered step.
- Order steps logically.
- Use imperative (command) statements, but avoid a demanding tone.
- Employ positive language whenever possible.
- Use parallelism for each statement.

See Appendix B for an example of a memo giving instructions.

Routine Claims and Adjustments

Routine claims—also called adjustments—occur in business when a customer asks for a refund, replacement, or exchange that the recipient will likely agree to. (Claims that require a persuasive argument will be discussed in Chapter 4.) Businesses are usually happy to clear up errors to preserve the business relationship with customers, so the direct approach is the appropriate organizing strategy for these messages.

When writing routine claims, follow this progression:

1. State the desired claim in a clear opening statement.
2. Provide justification for the situation in the body. Include order numbers, names of people spoken to, amounts of transactions, or any other identifying data that will help the receiver act. Keep a neutral tone.
3. Conclude with the specific action you desire and an end date. Use positive language to preserve goodwill.

See Appendix B for an example of a routine claim.

Appreciation and Goodwill

Relationship building is an important aspect of anyone's career, and sending goodwill messages to colleagues, employees, clients, customers, or others shows that you are an empathetic and thoughtful individual.

Show appreciation by sending a thank-you message when you receive a gift or experience hospitality. Write a goodwill message to acknowledge the receipt of an award, to recognize a job well done, or a promotion. Handwritten notes are the most personal way to express thanks and can be written on company letterhead or on elegant, simple stationery. Situations calling for a more businesslike goodwill message are best sent in an e-mail or a letter.

Use the direct strategy for appreciation or goodwill messages. Begin with the main point:

Thank you for opening your beautiful home to our staff for the annual company holiday party.

Congratulations on the birth of your new daughter, Sarah Ann! As a father myself, I know the joys awaiting you and Maureen.

Our staff has been eagerly implementing the new time saving techniques you presented in your recent workshop.

Include specific details about the situation in the body to show you are writing more than a generic thank-you and avoid overblown, exaggerated claims.

Most noteworthy, the billing department has already increased its output by 20 percent due to the new electronic filing system you created.

Not

The staff has been amazed by how much time they are already saving because of your awesome electronic filing system!

End with sincere words and avoid clichés such as *Best luck in the future.* Send goodwill messages in a timely manner and keep them short. See Appendix B for an example of a thank you e-mail.

Conclusion

Much of your day-to-day writing will be routine and will therefore conform to a direct writing strategy. There are many types of routine messages including requests, responses, claims, adjustments, and goodwill. Choosing the right channel for routine messages—e-mail, letter, memo, or texting—depends on the urgency and formality of the message itself. These everyday messages require a high degree of clarity and conciseness and therefore can be surprisingly challenging to write.

CHAPTER 4

Persuasive and Bad News Messages

Not all workplace communication delivers good or routine news to an audience happy (or at least willing) to hear from the writer. In the workplace, organizations must often convey messages that the audience may not wish to hear. Some of these messages require persuasion to accomplish their purpose. Other times, these messages must deliver unwelcome news in a way that is digestible to the reader. Both of these situations demand a different writing approach than the direct strategy we have discussed.

In general, an **indirect strategy** is used when the reader may feel uninterested, displeased, disappointed, or hostile about the message.[1] For example, customers may be less than interested in reading unsolicited sales messages; therefore, the situation calls for persuasion. Likewise, news that will negatively impact the reader may result in displeasure, disappointment, or anger. In the following sections, we will tackle how to write effectively for these common workplace scenarios.

Writing Persuasive Messages

Persuasive messages are written to gain agreement or win support for an idea. When an audience needs to be convinced to take some action, the first step is to examine the situation from the reader's point of view. As a writer, you must consider the question the reader will ask, which is, *What's in it for me?*[2] This means you must emphasize the benefits to the reader, an approach sometimes referred to as the *you* view. The *you* view, simply put, is not focusing on *me* (i.e., the writer or the organization). It shows respect for the audience by anticipating and understanding its needs and poses information in a way that will be meaningful to the reader (you) rather than the organization or writer (me).

Focusing on the benefits to the reader means that you must think strategically. For example, say you work for an auto repair chain that is trying to increase its customer base. In the message, you must emphasize the benefits of using your service. To determine the benefits, you examine the features you provide, such as being open late or having full service seven days a week. These features have inherent benefits. The benefit of being open late is that customers can pick up their cars after work. The benefit of being open every day is that customers can choose when to have a service performed. Focusing on benefits is the key to persuasive writing.

As mentioned, most situations calling for persuasive writing use an *indirect strategy*. This organizational style differs from the direct strategy in that it does not start off with the news or main idea. Instead, it builds toward that message using a series of calculated steps:

- The *opening* that captures reader attention
- The *body* that builds reader interest
- The *closing* that motivates reader action

The most common style of the indirect strategy for persuasion uses the AIDA model as illustrated in Table 4.1.

Table 4.1 AIDA persuasive strategy

Writing goal	Writing strategy
A Attract *attention*	Ask an arresting question Empathize with audience's concerns Forge common ground in a statement reader and writer agree on Mention an audience benefit Offer a compliment or praise
I Build *interest*	Provide acts, statistics, examples, or details relevant to reader Reduce resistance by anticipating objections Establish the value of a proposal Employ both logical and emotional appeals
D Increase reader *desire*	Spell out reason to act
A Ask reader to take *action*	Tell reader what action is requested Weave reader benefit into request

Persuasive messages need to immediately **attract attention** or they may be ignored. We do this in various ways. For example, if writing a persuasive fundraising letter to alumni, you might begin with a question that will stir up memories for the reader and likely make the reader want to read on: *Remember when you walked into your first college class not knowing what to expect?*

You may choose to open by establishing common ground by empathizing with the audience's concerns, thus: *We have all experienced the difficulty of finding parking near our offices.*

Another way to open a persuasive message is to forge common ground in a statement both reader and writer agree on: *The recent recession has taken a toll on middle-class families.*

In a sales message, you may want to focus on a reader benefit: *A free bottle of wine delivered monthly is just one of the many benefits you'll experience as a member of the Stonebrook Vineyard Wine Club.*

Offering a compliment or praise is another way to draw in a reader: *As a former Bruin whose thriving business is legendary among current UCLA business students, your success story would be an inspiration to the Accounting Association.*

Next, we need to **build interest** so our audience will stay with us. This can be accomplished with one or several of the following approaches:

- Using facts, statistics, examples, or details relevant to the reader
- Reducing resistance by anticipating reader objections
- Establishing the value of a proposal
- Employing both logical and emotional appeals

The following example uses a combination of these tactics.

Over the last two years, we are proud that our company has grown from 12 to 45 employees. However, while our staff was increasing, the number of parking spaces allocated to our suite has been steadily decreasing.

After interest has been built, the next step is to **increase reader desire** so your reader will act in the way you wish. In a sales letter, you might offer a money-back guarantee, free sample, or other incentives. If attempting to convince a boss, you'd want to include facts or other evidence that convincingly support your request.

To help you spend more time at home and at work and less time searching for parking, we've developed a new carpool plan. Beginning March 3, we will provide preferred parking spots to employees forming car-or vanpools of three or more.

Finally, **ask the reader to take action**. Be specific; set deadlines or limit the amount of time the offer is available. And don't forget to show gratitude!

Please let me know if you can speak at our meeting by August 20 so I can make the appropriate arrangements. You can phone me at (310) 544-2181 or e-mail me at jleastman@aol.com if you have any questions. I hope to see you in September!

Writing persuasively is an art, as any copywriter knows. Good persuasive writing always focuses on the readers' needs to attain the writer's ultimate purpose.

Types of Persuasive Messages

Common workplace situations call for persuasion, and although each message is built upon the AIDA model, specific scenarios demand fine-tuning to meet the writing objective.

Claims or Requests for Adjustments

Claims or requests for adjustments are written when things go wrong—an incorrect product was shipped, a bill is in error, merchandise is faulty, or an insurance or other claim must be filed. In most cases these kinds of messages can be dealt with by using the direct approach. However, if the writer expects foot-dragging on the part of the receiver or if prior requests have been ignored, the indirect strategy may work best.

Persuasive requests should present an honest argument that appeals to the audience's intelligence. The request should be posed using logic and facts in a moderate tone. The following paragraphs demonstrate the tone and content of a persuasive request.

> *Harper Hardware has a reputation for selling excellent products and providing personal service, and I have been a loyal customer for many years.*
>
> *I visited your store on September 3 to purchase a ceiling fan. The one I chose was sold out, so I decided to shop elsewhere. Before I left, the sales representative helping me called her manager, Fred Kroll, who suggested that I order the fan and have it shipped to my home at no extra charge. However, when the fan arrived and I examined the invoice, I saw I was charged $49.50 for shipping fees. Because I was promised the product without the fee, would you reimburse me for the charge on my credit card?*
>
> *I have every confidence you will take care of this matter and look forward to a satisfactory resolution.*

Favor Request

Many times you will need to ask favors of an organization or an individual. Such favor requests require persuasive writing. Begin by grabbing the reader's attention with a compliment or a benefit. Build interest by providing the details using the *you* view. Reduce resistance by providing reader benefits, and close by giving a specific action you'd like the reader to take. Don't forget to be courteous and show gratitude.

See Appendix B for a sample persuasive e-mail favor request.

Promoting an Idea

Supervisors often need to sell an idea to staff; likewise, staff members sometimes need to sell an idea to supervisors. Such persuasive messages that promote an idea need to be carefully worded. Say you work at a nonprofit organization and want to suggest creating a newsletter to help keep members involved. You need to provide facts to support your argument and make a strong case for how the newsletter would benefit the organization. This would require a description of the reason for the newsletter, facts supporting its usefulness, benefits of adopting the idea, and counter-arguments for possible objections to the idea. The document would end with a respectful conclusion stating the desired action and restating the main benefits.

See Appendix B for a sample of a persuasive memo promoting an idea.

Sales and Marketing Messages

As a consumer, you are frequently bombarded by unwanted sales and marketing messages whether they arrive in the mail, your inbox, your voice mail, or other means. But sales messages are a fact of life, and the fact is that they can work to meet an organization's objectives.

In larger organizations, writing sales messages is frequently delegated to an individual skilled in copywriting or to an outside vendor who specializes in these types of messages. However, in smaller organizations, you may be called upon to write convincing sales or marketing messages. In these cases, follow the AIDA organizational strategy. If sending out an e-mail, write a catchy subject line that encourages the reader to open the message. Begin your message with a statement that will grab your reader's attention and follow up with the details that will entice your reader to do what you want (*act now, call now, order now*, etc.). A caveat: Be sure to never misrepresent a product, service, or benefit or promise what you cannot deliver. It's unethical and bad business.

See Appendix B for a sample e-mail sales message.

Writing Negative or Bad News

Delivering unwanted news is a fact of life in the world of work, and when an organization must inform its stakeholders of negative news, there are basic goals that a message must attain:

- Confirm that the bad news will be understood and accepted
- Deliver the message in a way that the reader will continue to look at the writer or organization in a positive light
- Minimize future contact with the writer or organization about the negative situation

In some cases, delivering bad news uses the direct strategy. For example, anyone who has ever received a rejection letter from a college (certainly bad news!) knows that the bad news comes in the first line. This is done so that the anxious student does not overlook the information. If you think your reader would prefer to read the bad news first or if the situation demands firmness, use the direct approach for bad news. Begin with the bad news itself, explain the reasons for the bad news in the body, and close politely but firmly.

However, bad news is frequently delivered using the indirect strategy. This structure has four main elements, as Table 4.2 illustrates.

Table 4.2 Bad news message: indirect strategy elements

Indirect strategy elements	Writing strategy
Neutral or buffer statement	Describe a point on which both parties can agree Express appreciation Begin with good news Offer praise
Reasons leading to message	Include details supporting the denial Omit apologizing Use positive language wherever possible
The negative or undesired news	Clearly state the bad news to eliminate any misunderstanding Deemphasize the bad news by placing it in a subordinate clause
Polite close	Aim to build goodwill by offering an alternative, if possible, or a simple forward-looking statement

Begin your negative news correspondence with a **buffer or neutral statement** about which both the writer and reader can agree: *The recent renovation of the University Club has made it a much sought-after venue.*

Alternately, you may wish to start with a statement of **appreciation**: *Thank you for your well researched proposal to include Mayweather House in this year's Giving Back® volunteer day.*

You can offer any **good news** that is part of the message (as long as it doesn't mislead the reader into thinking the message contains all good news) or offer praise to open your bad news message: *All departments have done a great job decreasing their operating budgets.*

Start the second paragraph of the bad news message by providing logical **reasons** leading to the bad news itself. Slip in the **bad news** in a subordinate clause, and never repeat it. Make sure the negative message is clearly stated so you don't create misunderstanding or encourage further communication. For example, following the previous buffer statement, our next sentence might read:

> *Since we have expanded our facility to accommodate parties of over 100 and added a gourmet chef, the number of organizations and individuals requesting to use the University Club for events has tripled. Our bylaws require that we give priority to members of the club before opening up our schedule to nonmembers, so we are unable to accommodate your request to use the Dean's Room on the date you have requested.*

The **closing** of the bad news message must be polite and promote goodwill to the reader, who has just heard unwelcome news. Avoid being too conciliatory by offering to provide "additional assistance" or to "call us if you have further questions." If you are able to offer an alternative, do so. For example, if you know that another facility is available to accommodate the faculty retreat mentioned earlier or you can hold it on a different day, say so. If not, simply end on a positive note: *Thank you for considering the University Club for your event, and we look forward to helping you in the future.*

See Appendix B for an example of a bad news letter.

Conclusion

Writing to audiences who are not interested or pleased to be hearing from you requires tactful and skillful word crafting. Whether you are called upon to write persuasively to convince readers to do something they may object to or to deliver negative news, you will have greater success by thinking about the needs and reactions of the reader to achieve the purpose for which you are writing.

CHAPTER 5

Social Media and Text Messages

Social media has become a part of our daily lives. Although the phenomenon began with individuals, it didn't take long for organizations to figure out that this new platform provided another avenue of communication. In fact, the two-way conversation that lies at the heart of social networking has become such an integral part of an organization's presence that it has created an entire new job classification: social media manager.

Writing for social media contexts—social networking and video sharing sites, blogs, wikis, chat rooms—requires skill and careful, consistent management. This chapter will focus on the most common types of writing found in social networking: blogs, microblogs, and social networking sites. Before we begin, however, let's discuss how and why social media works.

Today's online audiences have come to expect that their opinions and voices be heard and acknowledged. No longer willing to absorb an organization's message passively, online audiences demand that an organization engage *with* them. Part of that engagement is conducted via the organization's social media presence on social networking sites, such as Facebook and LinkedIn, where consumers can post their reactions, comments, or opinions, and in blogs and microblogs, which try to garner large followings to promote a brand or awareness.

Large enterprises and small businesses alike have jumped on the social media bandwagon. Intel, a leader in social media use, has an extensive online presence that encourages managers, vendors, and others in the organization who have completed social media training to engage with stakeholders. Intel has an entire division devoted to managing its online presence, which it uses to build brand loyalty.

Small businesses and groups have also adopted social media in increasing numbers. For those with limited public relations and advertising budgets, social networking provides an excellent way to build a brand or increase a customer base. By connecting and engaging with stakeholders, small businesses, nonprofits, and other groups extend their reach in ways that were unheard of just a few years ago.

Social Media Audience Analysis

Social media has three main audiences: customers and clients, employees, and the media.

Customers and Clients

Current or potential customers and clients are a primary audience for social networking sites, blogs, and microblogs. People interested in an organization, a product, an issue, or a person form the target audience for much of social media. These readers are a niche audience actively looking for information and for engagement.

To best reach an organization's current and potential customers or clients, potential readers should be well defined. As with all writing tasks, writing for social media will be most effective if the content fits the needs and wants of the target audience. A good way to create a more intimate and successful relationship with your social media audience is to create one or several *personas* for these messages. A persona is a profile or an invented biography of a typical user or reader based on real audience analysis and data. For example, a university might create several personas as targets for social networking that could include newer alumni, older alumni, prospective students, or parents. Each persona has specific needs that could be targeted in the posts.

It's also a good idea to monitor the activity of your competitors' social media to understand your audience. By watching the discourse between a competitor and its audience, you may gain important feedback that will influence your own communication.

Employees

Large organizations use social media internally to provide spaces for colleagues to share knowledge. These in-house channels of communication have become extremely useful ways to connect coworkers, especially in organizations with multiple locations. Internal social media is often unavailable to outsiders.

Media

The traditional media is another audience for an organization's social media. News editors and writers comb the web in search of ideas for stories, interesting people, and news about organizations. Social media conversations provide the media with fodder for good copy, thereby allowing an organization to reach an otherwise fickle audience. And for unknown organizations, using free networking can be a way to attract the media's attention. By following a social media community's comments about a product or an organization, the traditional media can pick up on a new trend and write about it. In the eyes of the media, simply having an audience validates an organization or its product.

Social Media Guidelines

Because social media encourages conversations with almost anyone, those conversations can devolve into a free for all with the potential to do a lot of damage to an organization. For this reason, many groups adopt social media guidelines. Intel was one of the first multinational organizations to do so and has made those guidelines available to the public.[1] They remain an excellent source for any group that wants to create rules for its own social media presence.

Intel's "Social Media Guidelines" have three main principles: *disclose, protect,* and *use common sense. Disclose* refers to being transparent and writing in the first person—Intel requires anyone using social media on its behalf to identify himself or herself as an Intel employee. Furthermore, disclosure involves being upfront about having a vested interest in the topic. Lastly, disclosure includes talking to readers as if the conversation were face to face, using a friendly tone that avoids sounding pedantic. The final element of the disclose principle urges authors to write about their area of expertise only.

Protect means that no employee may violate confidentiality or legal guidelines. It serves to remind an organization's social media authors that writing online means writing on the record. This portion of the Intel's guidelines also bars slamming the competition and urges writers to be judicious about what they share.

Using common sense includes three points, the first of which is that social media must add value rather than take up space. This principle includes the idea that once authors have started an engagement, they must stay engaged, that is, not drop the ball. The final principle guiding Intel's social media use includes keeping a cool head and being careful and considerate. It also declares that mistakes should be admitted.

If your organization uses social media, you should create clear guidelines for all involved.

Blogs and Microblogs

Blogs and microblogs work hand in hand. Often a microblog announces the presence of a blog, which contains the meat of the message. Here we'll discuss the purpose and content of composing in these media.

Blogs

Blogs—short for *web logs*—are actually websites with individual posts archived by date in reverse chronological order. Blog posts tend to be articles, reviews, white papers, or recommendations, but almost all have a bias or voice the author's opinion. Because blogs are so plentiful, they must contain relevant information that appeals to readers and invites an interactive experience. Therefore part of each message usually includes a link to video clips, photographs, other blogs, websites, or an invitation to post comments. Blogs differ from a website in that they are dynamic and change frequently.

Many blogs are the work of one author. However, it is not unusual for a blog to have multiple contributors, thus keeping the content voice fresh. News entities, corporations, government agencies, and individuals all produce blogs.

The media is a major player in the blogosphere. Established media like *The New York Times* and *Fortune* magazine, for example, have blogs whose content is written by a staff writer or a contributor with expertise on a topic. For example, a reporter who covers medicine for *The New York Times* may also contribute blog posts on medical-related topics. The articles differ from the blog posts, which are less formal, contain the writer's opinion, and offer a link to a source. The news story published in the newspaper will be written in a more objective tone and may attribute a source but will not link directly to that source.

Organizations use blogs to communicate directly with consumers by offering useful, consistent, and interesting updates. Interactive blogs can be highly effective channels of communication that produce a lot of bang for a relatively low cost. When consumers sign up to follow a blog, for example, they may share that information with their own network of friends. By doing so, the number of people exposed to the information can expand exponentially. It is this characteristic that makes blogs so popular with organizations.

Individuals are responsible for a huge number of blogs. Some are read by a handful of friends and family; others end up creating new careers for the authors. Julie Powell's blogs about her cooking experiences of every recipe in Julia Child's *Mastering the Art of French Cooking* lead to a book and a movie, *Julie and Julia*. Before that Powell was a typical 20-something New Yorker.

Blogs frequently use RSS technology (*Rich Site Summary*, also dubbed as *Really Simple Syndication*), which allows followers to keep track of a website. An RSS feed is a software application that aggregates syndicated content. When an author syndicates content, readers may sign up to follow those headlines, posts, or updates. Since a blog's goal is often to accrue followers who sign up to follow it, blog writers incorporate searchable words and terms into the copy.

Characteristics of Blog Writing for the Workplace

Blogs written for business, government, or nonprofit organizations can take many shapes. Many if not most are written using the *inverted pyramid organizational style*. That is they begin with a paragraph that summarizes the main point. All details supporting that point are then arranged in descending order of importance and contain the 5Ws and 1H of journalism: who, what, where, when, why, and how. Figure 5.1 illustrates the inverted pyramid organizational style.

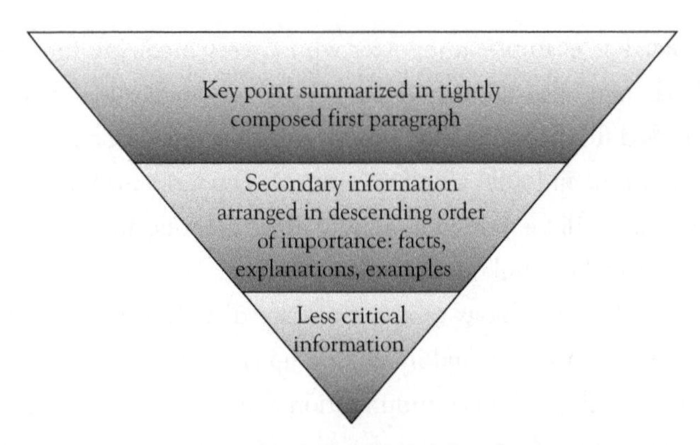

Figure 5.1 Inverted pyramid organizational style

Some blogs are written in a style that humanizes the dialogue between a company and its stakeholders. Consequently, the writing voice is more casual. In fact, some blogs read like a conversation with someone who has a distinctive voice. To capture that voice, using graphical elements (such as underlining, italics, or dashes) or turns of phrase that helps the blog sound like a conversation is not just allowed—it's expected. Look at the use of first person and casual language in this paragraph from Kevin Smith's post on *Business Insider's* blog:

> Over the weekend at the SXSW Interactive conference in Austin, I had the opportunity to briefly try on Google's next-generation gadget, Google Glass. The experience was interesting, to say the least .... The current design is dorky, but hopefully before they ship, Google can make Glass sleeker and not so noticeable.[2]

Organizations use blogs to promote themselves or their brands. However, experts advise against the temptation to try to sell to readers or sound overly promotional.[3] Notices of sweepstakes, coupons, special offers, or contests should comprise no more than 10 percent of what the audience sees. Instead, the organization should focus on informative content, engaging conversation, links, and infographics.

Blog post content falls into several broad types, as follows:

1. Narrative: Tells a story or provides an analogy to engage readers while explaining a concept or complex process.

2. Interviews: Transcribes or summarizes points from an interview with an expert on a topic.
3. Events: Describes an event the organization participated in or hosted.
4. Informational: Discusses a relevant topic to the audience.

The screenshot in Figure 5.2 shows a post from one of the National Institute of Health's (NIH) blogs and is a good example of an informational article. You can read the entire post at the Community Health Maps website.[4] http://communityhealthmaps.nlm.nih.gov/2014/06/30/how-accurate-is-the-gps-on-my-smartphone/

Figure 5.2 Information blog post

Source: Community Health Maps.com[5]

Before jumping in and writing a blog, spend some time observing the online community's conventions. Look for commonly used acronyms, jargon, and stylistic elements such as tone and language use. If you're going to become a member of a group, you don't want to stick out—you want to fit in.

Consider including the elements listed in Table 5.1 when you write a blog.

Table 5.1 Characteristics of blogs

Characteristics
Catchy, intriguing headlines
Keywords that contain blog's main idea; searchable words for Search Engine Optimization (SEO)
Graphical devices such as *italics*, dashes (—), and punctuation marks (!) for emphasis or to emulate a real conversation
Length of 300 to 400 words or more divided into paragraphs
Time and date stamp
Short sentences that avoid long introductory phrases or dependent clauses
One-sentence paragraphs or very short paragraphs
Questions
Blogrolls or hyperlinks of lists to other blogs
Casual tone with relaxed adherence to conventional grammar (but no glaring errors that would poorly reflect on professionalism)
Tags, keyword identification
Careful balance of information-share and self-promotion
Brief author bio and photo or other way to identify author
Artwork or some sort of graphic for visual interest

Microblogs

Microblogs are shorter than traditional blogs. They may be published using technologies other than the web-based methods, including text messaging, instant messaging, e-mail, or digital audio. Among the most notable microblog services are Twitter and Tumblr.

The popular Twitter microblogs called *tweets* are limited in length to 140 characters. With more than 270 million monthly users, Twitter has become increasingly popular with organizations as a way to reach a network instantly, thus creating word-of-mouth publicity. Social networks allow a message to be viewed instantly by thousands and thousands of readers, making the posts invaluable.

Tweeting has become commonplace at many organizations. Recently CEOs at Yahoo and Sun Microsystems tweeted notice of their firing, shooting out the message to their large networks in the time it took to type a few words. Smaller businesses, however, have mixed reactions about the effectiveness of tweets, perhaps because of the time factor involved in constant tweeting.[6]

There is no question, however, that Twitter fuels our celebrity culture. From Justin Bieber to President Barack Obama, celebrities dominate the TweetoSphere. In the summer of 2012, comedian Louis C.K. tweeted his followers about a relatively unknown comic, Tig Notaro. After the tweet, Notaro achieved instant celebrity status. So it is clear that tweeting can harness enormous power if a network is wide enough—and if the content is noteworthy.

Characteristics of Microblogs

Microblogs help an organization create an online presence. Those who follow a Twitter account, for example, are interested in a particular subject, and therefore, anticipate tweets as a way of keeping posted and up to the minute. The way people follow topics is through a unique characteristic of microblogs called *hashtags*, a word or phrase preceded by the # symbol that marks a topic by use of keywords. Hashtags make microblogs searchable and create the phenomenon known as *trending*. When a topic catches on and grabs the attention of many followers in a short time, that topic is said to be trending.

But because tweets are limited by length, they share certain characteristics, listed in Table 5.2.

Table 5.2 Characteristics of microblogs

No headline
Profile picture or company logo or photo of an individual's face or a product, subject to change if one doesn't produce results
Questions to prompt engagement
Length of up to 140 characters or roughly 12 words
Truncated language that omits articles (*a*, *an*, *the*) and abbreviations
Link to a recommended URL using a URL shortener such as bitly
Content containing response to another tweet, a recommendation, or link to an item of interest
Hashtags relevant to the topic
Punctuation marks "!" and "?"
Writing style similar to news headlines

Social Networking Sites

Another social media tool that has gained popularity among businesses is a social network page, with Facebook being the current favorite. Social networking sites should be considered complementary to an organization's online identity, not a replacement for it. Some consider the sites to be information gathering tools to measure marketing efforts rather than messaging tools—Facebook, for example, offers organizations considerable tools to measure involvement. We'll discuss two dominant social networking sites in the following sections.

Facebook

Facebook pages allow organizations to supplement their online presence by engendering interactivity among *fans* or readers. Organizations use this free new media to keep a community engaged as well as to drive traffic to their websites.

Facebook pages help brand an organization and are yet another way to communicate with stakeholders. They mirror blogs and tweets in that they, too, are conversational, interactive, and provide pertinent information to readers. Groups manage their Facebook pages by regularly updating wall posts written for *news feed optimization*. Essentially this means that the content encourages fans to *like* or post comments. The more *likes* a posting receives, the more probable it is that Facebook's algorithm will pick up the post and put it in a news feed. When that happens, more readers will receive the post, theoretically increasing the audience. Comments or likes posted on Facebook pages also help an organization gauge what's going right—or wrong! For example, Dr. Pepper Snapple Group learned that its Facebook followers preferred edgy one-liners instead of special offers and prices as a result of issuing the message on its Facebook page.[7]

When composing an organization's Facebook page, writers should employ the language used on all social media and corporate communications for branding purposes and to stay on message. Notice how this small business posts information on its Facebook page in the screenshot shown in Figure 5.3.

Figure 5.3 Santa Barbara School of Performing Arts Facebook page

LinkedIn

Considered the best social networking site for attracting employees, LinkedIn company pages connect a business with the millions of people who have profiles on the professional networking site. LinkedIn company pages allow an organization to post company news, business opportunities, and job openings. Such pages can provide job seekers with a look inside an organization so they can better evaluate whether their skills fit with the organization's culture and needs.

Integrate the characteristics listed in Table 5.3 when writing status updates.

Table 5.3 Characteristics of LinkedIn status update

Wording consistent with other organizational messages for branding
Messages relevant and posted on a regular basis
Tone that is conversational, wording is concise
Links, images, and videos that are embedded
Updates sent at the beginning or end of a regular business day

Conclusion

Social media has become essential for an organization's online presence. Organizations using all social media must track postings, respond to inquiries, delete damaging or inflammatory comments, and post regularly, making its management time consuming. Writing clearly with the organization's goals and values in mind is important to all social media messages. The employee adept at using social media will be a valuable member of any organization.

PART III

Reports and Presentations

CHAPTER 6

Reports

Reports provide accounts of information and range from short, informal e-mails to over 100 page formal manuscripts. They may be distributed to an internal or external audience, read via hard copy or on a computer screen, and written in a variety of business genres.

Typically reports fall into one of several categories. **Informational reports** present information without analysis. They offer facts but do not interpret information. **Analytical reports** interpret data or information and often provide recommendations. They may be written to assess a business opportunity, provide solutions to problems, or to support business decisions. Proposals are analytical reports that pose persuasive requests to influence decisions either within an organization or to an external audience.

Reports, like all professional communication, must be well written: clear, comprehensive, and organized. In addition, because they often contain information obtained from a wide variety of sources, reports must be meticulously cited to give them credibility. This chapter provides an overview of the most common types of reports, the various formats used to present reports, components to include in reports, and document design.

Report Types

Whether informal or formal, short or long, each type of report has a specific purpose. Individual organizations may name reports differently, but most reports fall into one of the categories listed in Tables 6.1 and 6.2.

Personnel in organizations write other types of reports. A few of the most common include the **strategic plan**, which defines a company's goals and objectives and the action plans to attain those goals. A **marketing plan** outlines an organization's target market and competition to best identify its own niche and presents the advertising and promotional plans

Table 6.1 Common informational reports

Report type or name	Purpose	Elements to include
Activity	Summarize regular activities or unusual events for managers	Bulleted points describing activities
Trip/development activity	Describe most important takeaway to justify trip or activity	Introduction, body, conclusion
Progress	Explain status of project, describing work completed, work in progress, work to do, current or anticipated problems, expected date of completion	Background, work completed, work in progress, problems, target completion date(s)
Technical	Provide managers with facts and data	Executive summary, introduction, conclusions, recommendations (if applicable)

Table 6.2 Common analytical reports

Report type	Purpose	Elements to include
Feasibility	Evaluate viability of specific course of action	Background, benefits, problems, costs
Proposal	Persuade audience to take a course of action	Letter of transmittal, abstract or executive summary, table of contents, list of illustrations, introduction, background, plan, schedule, personnel, budget
Recommendation	Justify action, often within an organization	Background, alternatives, recommendation
White paper	Argue a position or propose a solution; provide evidence of subject expertise	Introduction, background, solution, conclusion

to maximize its market share. A **business plan** is a roadmap for a new enterprise or a formalized plan for growing an existing business.

Report Styles

Whether a report is **formal** or **informal** depends on the audience. Many internal reports—those written for someone within an organization—will be informal. For example, if a supervisor asks an employee to write up a justification for taking a trip, the report would likely be informal, written as an e-mail or a memo and using a casual, conversational tone. Not all reports written for internal audiences are informal, however. If a division of a large organization must submit a yearly strategic plan to corporate headquarters, the report would likely be a bound or digital manuscript written in a formal tone. In fact, such a report is among the most formal type of writing done in organizations.

One of the ways to hit the right note of formality is by employing the characteristics of formal and informal writing. Refer to Table 1.4 (Formal and informal writing styles) for a breakdown of the characteristics and components of each writing style.

Report Formats

Reports may be written using a variety of document formats. For example, a report informing a manager about a trip to an industry expo might be delivered in a short **e-mail**. Sometimes, a formal **letter** may be used. Say a company is responding to a request for information about providing drought-resistant landscaping services. The initial inquiry may have come via phone or e-mail, but a reply detailing the services the company offers would be best communicated in a formal letter. Such a document would likely be several pages in length.

Memos are also effective for presenting information in reports. Memo reports tend to be less lengthy and less formal than manuscripts, ranging from one to several pages, and are typically used within an organization, though they may at times be sent to an outside audience. Memo reports are often sent via e-mail and are accompanied by a brief e-mail message that forecasts the document's contents (see transmittal messages section that follows). **Manuscript** reports may be produced in print or digital versions. Print manuscripts are bound; digital versions of the print report are often a PDF of the print version. Some digital reports contain links that take the reader outside of the manuscript.

Today many companies prefer **report decks** over more traditional reports. Report decks (sometimes referred to as data blocks) are created in PowerPoint and include narrative and graphics to present information succinctly. They are distributed digitally to individuals or groups, and although they are prepared using presentation software such as PowerPoint, they are not designed to be used for oral presentations.[1]

See Appendix B for sample documents of a trip report e-mail, a memo proposal, and a letter report.

Report Components

Reports often contain an assortment of elements, which are broken into major sections: front matter, body, and back matter. Here we'll discuss the various elements that may be included in a report.

Transmittal

Whether being distributed digitally or presented in person, reports are always accompanied by an introductory message called a transmittal. The transmittal accompanies the report but is not part of the report itself. The message may be in the form of a letter, especially for formal reports going to an outside audience, but it may also be an e-mail or a memo. Transmittals are written using the direct strategy and discuss what the report is about and why it was written. They may introduce the main points of interest within the report. The more formal the report, the more formal the transmittal.[2]

Front Matter

Front matter is comprised of the first few pages of a report that come before the narrative. Front matter may include a **cover**, an attractively designed front piece for formal reports and those intended for a wide audience. The written information on a cover varies, but it will, at a minimum, contain the title of the report and the name of the person or organization submitting it.

Some reports contain an **abstract**, a brief distillation of the report's content. Scientific or technical reports often contain abstracts. *Descriptive abstracts* simply describe the information in the report without offering interpretation. *Informative abstracts* summarize key results and offer interpretations.

A **title page** will contain some or all of the following:

- Report name
- Person or organization submitting the report
- Name of individual receiving the report
- Date the report is submitted
- Copyright

The **table of contents** is an outline of the report that provides readers with the location of major categories and subcategories of information. A good table of contents should offer enough detail so the reader can immediately locate a particular section. Such detail may be written in several formats:

- Decimal outline format (1.0, 1.1, 1.1.2, etc.)
- Alphanumeric outline (I, A, 1, a, etc.)
- Graphic markers (boldface, indentation, etc.)

Obviously, a table of contents must contain accurate pagination.

The **list of illustrations** shows all tables, figures, and maps. It appears on its own page and is not part of the table of contents. Tables are generally listed and numbered separately from other figures. All other figures (charts, graphs, maps, photographs) are listed sequentially as they appear in the report. (We will discuss the types of illustrations and the rules for inserting them into reports later in this chapter.)

An **executive summary** presents the most important elements of a report in a condensed form so a busy manager can glean the report's most critical takeaways. Depending on the length of the report, an executive summary may be one or 10 pages. For longer executive summaries, informational headings should be used. Executive summaries are objective and must accurately summarize information contained in the report body. A well-constructed executive summary often makes reading the entirety of the report unnecessary.

Body

The body of a report contains several sections. The **introduction** orients the reader. It includes background information explaining the context of the report and defines the report's limitations (what it will and will not cover). It may provide an overview or the report's organization, sources or methodology used to conduct research, definitions of key terminology, authorization for writing the report, and the report's purpose or significance. An introduction should not be confused with a summary, which is read in lieu of or separately from a report body.

The **findings** include the information and supporting facts of the report. Reports are broken into sections or chapters defined by **headings**. Whichever system is used—alphanumeric or decimal outline or graphics for reader cues—headings are organized by hierarchy (see the sample below). *First level headings* name major topics. *Second level headings subdivide* information under a first level heading. *Third level headings* further subdivide information. It is not necessary to give each body paragraph its own heading; doing so can bog down the reading of a long report. However, for readability, include at least one heading per page.

The following is a sample of headings using graphic markers.

TITLE
(Centered, caps, boldface)
Heading Level 1
(Centered, upper and lower case, boldface)
Heading Level 2
(Flush left, upper and lower case, boldface)
Heading Level 3
(Flush left, upper and lower case, boldface, begin typing directly after heading)

Headings may be informative or descriptive. Informative headings can be written as questions or as summaries, but they are most effective when they are limited to four to eight words.[3] Descriptive headings name topics.

In the various sections of a report, information is often cited using a formal **citation system**. Academic reports use discipline specific citation systems such as MLA for the humanities, APA for the social sciences, or CSE for the sciences. Many organizations use *The Chicago Manual of Style* (CMS) as their guide for citing, which employs footnotes or endnotes accompanied by a list of references in the report's back matter.

It is important to consider the ethical use of information at this point. It is dishonest (and illegal!) to use copyrighted material without permission from the author. You may not use photographs or other images you encounter on the Internet without specific permission. The only exception to this rule is information published by the government.

Another element of ethical use of information is the avoidance of plagiarism. Never cut and paste information and claim it as your own work. Instead, rely on paraphrase and summary, using direct quotes only when they add emphasis, and always with proper attribution. Whether paraphrasing, summarizing, or quoting, always give credit to your sources; it makes your work appear well researched as well as making it ethical.

All reports must have an ending. A **summary** is a recap of the report findings. **Conclusions** explain how the data in the findings relate to the original problem named in the report's introduction. Because conclusions sum up the report's details, they never contain new material. Some reports end with **recommendations**. Recommendations provide solutions to the problem the report addresses or suggestions for future actions. Sometimes report conclusions and recommendations appear in the same section.

The following example shows the differences between a finding, a conclusion, and a recommendation.

Finding More than 80 percent of pet owners delay prophylactic dental treatment for their pets, citing cost as the deterrent.

Conclusion Current high costs for prophylactic pet dental treatment are leading to more costly and serious pet health issues and unhappy pet owners.

Recommendation Develop alternate fee structures for prophylactic dental treatments.

Back Matter

Back matter is the section of a report that contains details referred to, but not fully included, in the body. Typical sections are the **references** and **appendixes**. References contain a list of the sources cited or consulted in the writing of the report, using a formal citation system. Appendixes are supplemental to the body of the report and are labeled *A*, *B*, *C*, and so on when more than one appendix is needed. Appendixes are reserved for lengthy or highly detailed portions of a report that readers may not want to read in detail.

Report Visuals

Visuals in reports serve several functions. First, they draw readers' attention. The old adage "A picture is worth a thousand words" is true. Whether a bar graph or pie chart, visuals turn numbers into pictures and help readers grasp points more readily. Second, they help break up text and make a long report more readable and visually attractive.

Visuals should only be used when they highlight an important point, and choosing the correct visual to communicate an idea or fact is crucial to relaying meaning. Table 6.3 summarizes the uses of the most commonly used visuals.

Table 6.3 Visual types and purpose

Type	Purpose or use
Table	Organize numerical data or information into rows and columns
Bar or column chart	Show data in vertical or horizontal columns for comparison
Gantt chart	Plan and track status of project with beginning and end dates
Line chart	Illustrate trends over time; compare data over time
Map	Show specific points within an area; illustrate distances; show geographic features
Organizational chart	Depict hierarchies within an organization; show how elements relate to one another
Photographs	Illustrate actual image; record events
Pie chart	Show parts of a whole adding up to 100%

Tables display information in rows and columns and can be comprised of text (such as Table 6.3) or numbers. Numerical tables are used to show large amounts of data and are easily created in spreadsheet or word processing software. Place tables with important information within the body of the narrative; place other tables in the appendix. When making tables, organize data logically, name row and column headings clearly, and use white space, gradation of color, or lines to differentiate between rows and columns.

Bar Charts are excellent ways to illustrate comparisons and are most useful to the reader when they communicate one simple message.

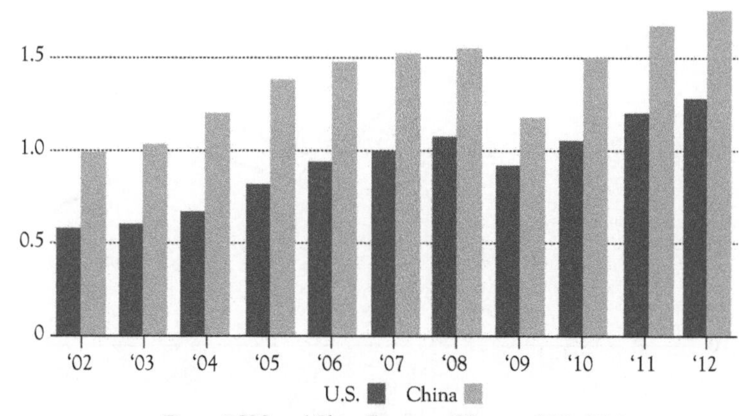

Figure 7. U.S. and China Exports and Imports 2002–2012
U.S.–China trade gap in dollars.
Source: National Association of Manufacturers

Figure 6.1 Sample bar chart

For example, Figure 6.1 shows the trade gap in the United States by comparing exports to imports. To help your reader readily grasp the meaning of the bar graph, use color, shade, or crosshatch to differentiate data. Label the horizontal and vertical axes using specific values that are clearly demarcated.

A **Gantt Chart** is a type of bar chart used as a project management tool. It shows the length of a project and names specific tasks to be accomplished, sometimes naming key players. Do a simple Google search to see examples of Gantt charts.

Line Charts are effective ways to show changes over time. They may contain one or several lines to show several elements of data. Figure 6.2 shows a comparison of gross sales between two divisions of an organization. Notice how the horizontal axis shows time and the vertical axis shows the dollar value.

Maps are useful ways to show geographic data with another feature or set of data. For example, a map may be used to show weather patterns across a region or a country, such as the one in Figure 6.3. A map's label must explain its purpose, and its caption must explain the map's features. Maps should only show the data that needs to be illustrated. For example, if you are using a map to show voting districts, don't include major highways, which are irrelevant to the map's main point.

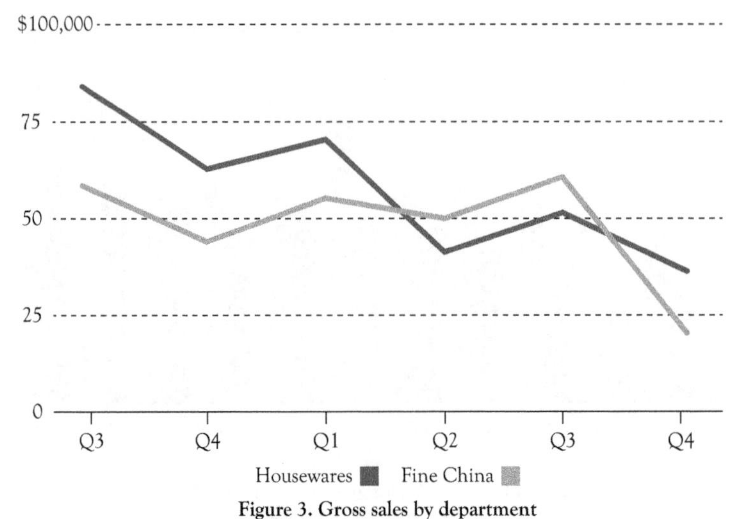

Figure 6.2 Sample line chart

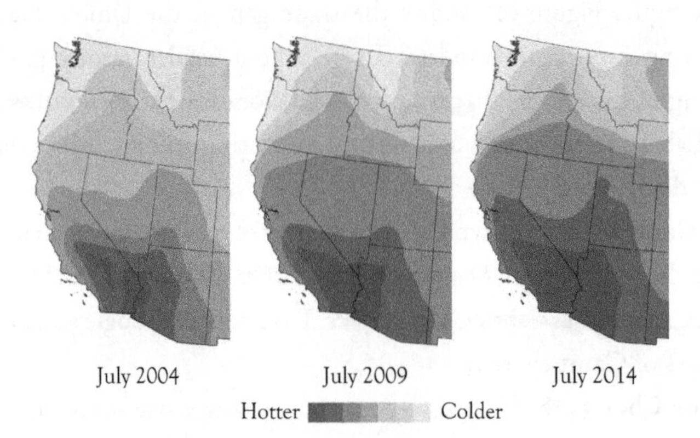

Figure 6.3 Sample map Average high temperatures

Organizational Charts show hierarchies within a group. They are easily created in most word processing software and include boxes with text. They are constructed using a top-down structure; the largest box at the top represents the highest level of authority. Smaller boxes may be used to indicate descending order of authority. Equivalent levels are placed horizontally.

Photographs should be used to convey a specific message or to illustrate a point. For example, if you are writing a brochure about poison oak, a photograph showing the distinctive three-leaf formation would be extremely helpful. Never simply capture a photograph from the Internet and use it. Many stock photo sites such as Shutterstock.com offer low-cost or even free use of photographs, with permission. And remember that unless a photograph has high enough resolution, it will appear fuzzy and will therefore be useless to the reader. The higher the dpi value (dots per inch), the higher the resolution and the greater the clarity of the photograph.

Pie Charts (or graphs) show data that adds up to 100 percent in wedges within a circle. They are an excellent way to help a reader visualize parts of a whole. For example, say you were creating an advertising budget for a campaign and wanted to illustrate where the funds were being spent, such as the sample in Figure 6.4. When making a pie chart, show the different sections in colors or patterns and group smaller percentages together in an *other* section.

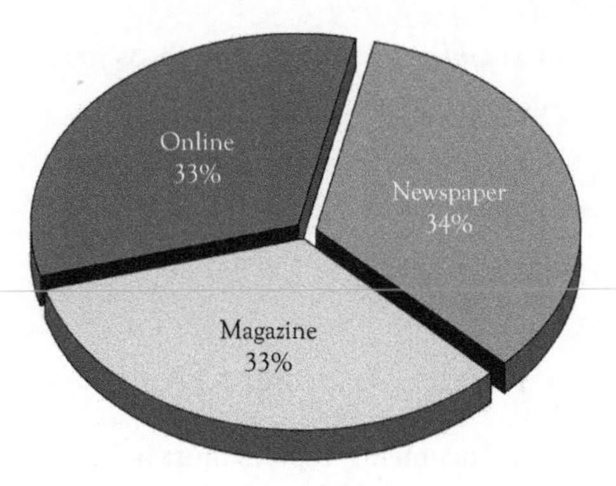

Figure 1. Advertising budget by media type

Figure 6.4 Sample pie chart

Infographics differ from the more conventional visuals previously discussed. They use images to tell a story, distill information, and provide a streamlined and alternative way to understand complex ideas. They employ elements of design to communicate visually. These creative images are interesting to look at and are used in many ways: presenting survey data, recruiting employees, showing how something works, and much more. But as arresting as these graphics are, they can be challenging to create. Many tools are available for creating infographics such as Piktochart and Visual.ly.

Integrating Visuals into Text

Use the following rules when integrating visuals into a report.

1. Mention the visual in the narrative. Direct your reader's attention to the visual by referencing it. Write "See Figure 1" or "As Figure 1 illustrates … ". Never let a visual stand alone without some discussion of its contents.
2. Place the visual near where it is discussed. Do not confuse readers by making them search for the image.
3. Label visuals clearly. The title of the visual should accurately and concisely describe its main message.
4. Use a caption with a title to identify the image's purpose.
5. Keep images on one page. Never break up a table or other image onto two pages.
6. Refer to tables as *tables* and all other images as *figures.*
7. Number visuals sequentially.
8. Include a source line when taking information from an outside source. Place it in the lower left.
9. Place lengthier visuals in an appendix.

Report Document Design

As with all workplace documents, reports must be easy to read, so document design is extremely important. For shorter reports—e-mails, letters, memos—the standard document design we have discussed earlier applies. Here we'll discuss document design for longer reports.

Page Design

The way your report page appears will encourage or discourage reading. These pointers can help make a long report more visually appealing.

1. Consider using an attractive **header and footer** as a way to create visual interest in longer reports. A logo or infographic image that is unobtrusive can liven up a page. Even a simple colored line across the top and bottom of a page will make a report with many pages appear less tedious. Include **page numbers** in either the header or footer.
2. Use right and left **margins** of 1 to 1.25 in., and use 1 in. for the top and bottom. You may also opt to use two columns for a standard report. Doing so can make dense text easier to track.
3. Choose font style for readability. Many manuscript reports use serif fonts, but increasingly, sans serif fonts are also being used. If you do use a sans serif font for a report, adjust your **spacing** between lines. When a report will be read on a screen, use generous spacing between lines with both serif and sans serif fonts. (Locate the Pew Research Center's report Millennials: A Portrait of Generation Next on the Internet for an excellent model of document design using a serif font to be read on the screen.)
4. Differentiate between body copy and headings with boldface and font size. If you use a sans serif font for body copy, choose a serif font for headings. Never use more than two fonts in a long report.
5. Add color for visual interest. Stick to a color scheme using no more than three complementary colors.

Writing Collaboratively

Because reports may be large projects, they are often written collaboratively. Producing a collaborative project on a deadline can be challenging. Different writing styles and abilities and even different levels of commitment to a project can affect collaborative writing. If you are working with a group of people to write a report, consider these pointers.

- Meet regularly to discuss project progress
- Assign tasks and keep on schedule
- Share information

- Use a group editing document space like Google Docs or Dropbox
- Rely on individual strengths
- Edit for a unified voice and document design

Conclusion

Reports are an important way of communicating information within organizations, to stakeholders, and to other organizations. Many types of reports are regularly written in the workplace using various formats, from short e-mails to manuscripts of more than 100 pages. Reports are broken into sections and must be well organized and visually appealing. Collaborative report preparation can expedite completion but requires commitment and coordination. Clearly written reports that display information in an approachable way continue to play a large role in communicating in the workplace.

CHAPTER 7

Presentations

You will likely be called upon to deliver presentations throughout your career. Presentations are considered a high stakes communication tool that influence an organization's constituencies and consequently play an important role in the workplace. Presentations may be given to an internal audience of employees, partners, boards, investors, or vendors, or to an external audience of customers, the media, analysts, or the community.[1] A presentation can be used for marketing, sales, training, or events and may be seen by one to thousands of people. Similarly, there are various types of presentations—informal or formal briefings, oral renditions of a written report, or even virtual presentations.

Master presenter Jean-luc Doumont breaks the creation of presentations into five steps:

1. Planning the presentation
2. Designing the presentation and defining its structure
3. Creating visuals that convey messages
4. Delivering the presentation
5. Answering questions and driving your point home[2]

We will discuss each of the five steps and how you can maximize the positive influence of your presentations.

Planning the Presentation

Begin planning your presentation by analyzing the **audience**. When your goal is to encourage people to listen to you and act upon what you say, you must connect with them and therefore understand them. Think about who will be hearing the presentation and answer these types of questions about your audience:

- What is important to the audience?
- What knowledge do they already have about the topic?
- What will motivate them to act?
- Who influences the audience?
- What are the audience's expectations of the presentation?
- What does the audience want?
- Why are they in attendance?
- What questions will they have?
- How do they feel about the presentation? (i.e., are they interested, uninterested, or even hostile?)

Next, define your presentation's **purpose**. Do you want employees to understand a new health plan? Are you presenting to land a sale or to deliver a proposal to a potential client? Are you speaking to inspire a group? When creating presentations, you must know what you want to achieve as a result of the presentation and focus your content on that goal.

Finally, you will want to assess the presenting situation. Where will it take place? Preparing a talk for a few people in a small conference room is quite different from speaking before an audience of 50 or more. Also consider the length of your presentation. How long will you be expected to speak? Awareness of your time limit will help you tailor your presentation.

Designing the Presentation and Defining Its Structure

Once you have examined your audience and purpose, it's time to think about defining the structure of your talk. Look at a presentation as having three elements: an **introduction**, **body**, and **conclusion**.

All presenting experts agree that you must begin your presentation by immediately engaging your audience. Advice about how to do so, however, varies. Some experts urge presenters to incorporate elements of storytelling into their talks. For example, if you were addressing a group of farmers, you might want to begin with a story of how one individual turned around his business by adopting a new type of crop rotation. The story you tell should resonate with your audience and grab its attention.

Another way to garner audience attention is to offer a promise. By hooking the audience with the idea that "By the end of this session, you'll know ten ways to improve your employees' productivity," you give listeners a reason to tune in. Likewise, you might start with a startling statistic, ask a provocative question, or relate a relevant news item. Keep in mind that whichever attention-grabbing device you use, your audience will always want to know what's in it for them. The following are examples of some attention-grabbing hooks:

This year, pet owners will spend an expected $60 billion on their animals. Today I'm going to show how you can grab a piece of that pie.

When was the last time you woke up and felt excited about going to work? I believe everyone should feel that every day, and that's what I'm here to talk to you about today.

The recent tragic news about social media bullying has every parent in America on alert. We're here today to make sure that doesn't happen in our town.

The meat or body of your presentation contains the information you want your audience to take away. Here expert opinions vary, as well. Some say audiences are only capable of taking away one main message, and there may be some truth in that assertion. Think of the last time you attended a lecture or a talk—how much do you actually remember about it? Others claim that the audience will recall up to three points.[3] In either case, you can see that bombarding an audience with fact after fact is not the way to create a successful presentation.

Once you have determined the primary takeaway(s) for your presentation, build the body of your talk and integrate smooth transitions to link ideas. You may want to develop a theme you can return to. For example, you could weave your introductory story throughout the presentation. In the case of the presentation to farmers we discussed earlier, you'd talk again about the farmer you described in your opening.

Remember that oral delivery of information differs from written delivery of information; written reports can be exhaustive, brimming with data and information. However, presenting requires persuasion and motivation to listen and recall, and the best way to attain these goals is to alternate between facts and stories that illustrate those facts. Never use a talk as a "data dump."[4]

Conclude your presentation by returning to your original message and recapping for your audience. Leave them with something to think about. If appropriate, open up the talk to questions, an excellent opportunity for you to drive home your point.

Create an outline of your talk and then write a script. Of course you will not read the script, but writing one will allow you to rehearse and time yourself.

Creating Visuals that Convey Messages

Today, the use of visuals (usually slides) to accompany a presentation is practically mandatory. Designing your presentation with images that will enhance rather than confuse or bore your audience is as important as what you say.

The use of presentation software such as PowerPoint, Prezi, or Keynote can be a double-edged sword. On the one hand, these products are designed to be easy to use—that's good for the unartistic presenter. However, because most of us are not designers and do not have training in visual design, we tend to create presentations that do not take into account audience needs and expectations. That's bad for your audience.

Think of the visuals you create as back-up support, not as an outline for you to follow. Words on slides should be kept to a minimum; the audience is coming to hear you, not read. Use images that convey meaning and that are adapted to the size of the room. Avoid the common pitfalls of poor design for presentation slides: cluttering slides with words or data, using a small font, including images of poor quality, using color unwisely, and incorporating annoying sound effects.

Follow these steps when designing your presentation:

1. **Keep slides simple**. Avoid clutter and don't be afraid of white space.
2. **Limit bulleted points and text**. The best slides may have no text at all; instead, they contain images that illustrate a point the speaker is

making. Stick to the 10-20-30 rule of PowerPoint developed by Guy Kawasaki: 10 slides, 20 minutes, 30 point font.[5]

3. **Limit animation and transitions**. Listeners will grow antsy with too much visual noise.
4. **Use meaningful graphics**. Photographs and charts must be of high resolution. Don't plan to use the same graphics you've used in a report; most charts and graphs that have a lot of detail do not work in presentations. Choose powerful images with high impact. If you make a point with your words, illustrate the point with a slide.
5. **Incorporate a visual theme**. Devise a consistent theme, but do not use commonly available templates. Audiences have seen them.
6. **Design your slides**. Use color well; create an appropriate, visually pleasing color theme and stick to it. Use a font that will be visible to all seeing the presentation.
7. **Incorporate video or audio**. The use of video and audio is a great way to change the pace of a presentation. However, if used, they should add value.[6]

Suggested Presentation Resources

The following is a short list of additional resources to assist you in presentation design.

Resonate by Nancy Duarte[7]
Slide:ology by Nancy Duarte[8]
"Really Bad PowerPoint" by Seth Godin[9]
Presentation Zen by Garr Reynolds[10]
The Naked Presenter by Garr Reynolds[11]

Delivering the Presentation

It's normal to be anxious when giving a presentation, and the single best way to avoid nervousness is to prepare. Practice, but do not memorize your talk. (You may want to memorize your outline, however.) Record yourself and rehearse with your visuals. If you can video yourself, better yet. Obtain feedback so you can make changes before you speak.

Follow these pointers when delivering a presentation:

1. **Maintain eye contact with your audience**. If you don't, you'll appear shifty. Look at different individuals as you speak, not just one person.
2. **Vary your tone**. No one will stay engaged with monotonous droning.
3. **Avoid "upspeak."** Inflecting your voice up at the end of a sentence that isn't a question will make audiences take you less seriously.
4. **Stand up straight**. Avoid shifting your weight from leg to leg.
5. **Find the right pace**. Not too fast; not too slow. It's easy to speed up when you're nervous, so consciously pace yourself.
6. **Remove all verbal static**. Audiences will tune out if your presentation contains ums, ahs, or other repetitive space-filling sounds.
7. **Look pleasant**. Watch yourself as you rehearse. Are you grimacing? Do you look petrified? The old saying, "Fake it until you make it" applies here. Just because you are nervous, doesn't mean you should *look* nervous!
8. **Dress the part**. Know what level of attire will be best received.
9. **Use movement strategically**. Only Chris Rock can get away with pacing across the stage. Stillness (that is not statuelike) connotes confidence. If you want to make a gesture, make it large and deliberate. And never turn your back on your audience!

Answering Questions and Driving Your Point Home

Many people who present dread opening up the conversation to questions, but that stance is counterproductive. The audience is not your enemy, and you have everything to gain by engaging with its members. Say you have given a sales presentation, and potential customers have a question after the presentation. Those people are interested enough in your product to learn more; but without answers to their questions, they will certainly not want to make the purchase. Look at the question period as the second half of your presentation and as an opportunity to drive home your message.

The best way to not fear a question and answer portion of a presentation is to anticipate questions in advance and prepare responses. This is especially true if you are delivering information that may be controversial. If an audience member asks a question about a thorny point or a perceived shortcoming, answer honestly.

To deal with questions effectively, follow these guidelines:

1. Listen to the question carefully.
2. Ask for clarification if necessary.
3. Repeat the question in your own words.
4. Answer the question concisely. If it's a straightforward answer, present it clearly. For more difficult questions, use a phrase such as "That is a difficult question to answer in a few words," or "I understand your frustration."
5. Check to see if the question has been fully answered.
6. Don't answer questions to which you do not know the answers or that need more time than you can give at that moment.
7. Limit the time frame for taking questions.
8. Invite further questions via e-mail, if appropriate.
9. Remain polite and in control.
10. End by thanking the audience.

Conclusion

Presentations are an important part of communicating in the workplace. Planning is the key to giving effective presentations. As you plan, analyze your audience and be clear about your own purpose and goal in giving the presentation. When preparing the content, remember that delivering information orally differs greatly from delivering it in text. Structure your talk by integrating stories to help make your point and to engage your audience. Design visuals to support you, the speaker. Finally, rehearse to minimize fear of presenting. After your presentation, consider a question period as an opportunity to reinforce your message and offer honest answers.

PART IV

Employment

CHAPTER 8

Employment Communication

Gone are the days of starting a career at a company and staying there until you retire. Today people change jobs between 10 and 15 times during their work lives.[1] That means keeping your employment documents up to date is a must. Today job searchers must be versatile and savvy about not only locating hidden or unadvertised jobs, but in their approach to applying to positions. This chapter will discuss the basic job search documents: cover letter, resume, reference list, thank-you note, and LinkedIn profile. Sample documents are also provided in Appendix B.

Cover Letters

A cover letter accompanies a resume and serves to introduce the job applicant, explain the candidate's strongest selling points and reason for wanting the position, and to ask for an interview. Cover letters are as important as resumes and are meant to persuade the reader that your skills and abilities can be an asset to the organization. Through carefully crafted sentences and precise word choice, the cover letter not only illustrates your ability to communicate; it highlights your qualifications and explains why you are a good fit for the job. Even if a job advertisement doesn't specifically ask for a cover letter, you show your professionalism by including one.

Today most cover letters are sent as an e-mail with the resume as an attachment. However, in some cases you may want to send a hard copy through the mail. In all cases, the cover letter must focus on the needs of the employer, not the job seeker. Speaking about how a job will help your career goals is hardly a good way to convince a potential employer (who is likely evaluating multiple candidates) of your ability to add value to the organization.

There are two types of cover letters: those for solicited jobs and those for unsolicited or unadvertised positions.

Cover Letters for Solicited Positions

The purpose of the cover letter for solicited jobs is to introduce the candidate's strongest qualifications and convince the reader to move to the resume. Job ads, whether found on a job board, an organization's website, or through other means, contain the minimum requirements and duties the job searcher needs to meet to be considered for the position. Your cover letter should convince the reader that you meet those requirements.

Although many times job ads do not contain a contact name, it behooves the job searcher to do a bit of research and locate the individual who will actually read the letter and resume. Always try to address the letter to an actual human being rather than to a generic *To Whom It May Concern* or *Dear Human Resources*. Such industriousness will pay off by showing you to be eager and resourceful.

Letters for solicited jobs use the direct strategy and contain the following elements.

Opening

If you have been referred to the job or if you know someone highly regarded by the organization, begin your cover letter by using that person's name. If not, begin by stating your interest in the position and how you heard about it. Include a statement of your strongest selling points for the position. Never write about how the job will benefit you; instead, provide evidence of how your skills and abilities will be of value to the company.

> Malcolm Esteban, a recruiter I met at Ohio State University's Career Day last month, suggested that I apply for the marketing internship at BC Industries. My experience with fundraising combined with my strong interpersonal skills and desire to enter the marketing field make me well suited for the summer internship.

> Your posting for an associate actuary on CareerBuilder.com interests me greatly. My degree in actuarial science and past experience working in risk assessment will be assets to Indiana Life.

Body

The body of the cover letter illustrates your suitability for the position in one or two paragraphs. Start body paragraphs with clear topic sentences, and provide actual examples rather than vague statements. For instance, if one of the job requirements is experience in customer relations, a good topic sentence might begin as follows: *My two years' experience as a customer relations representative at a busy department store has allowed me to use my positive attitude and tact in many challenging situations.* More details could readily follow.

The body can also be a chance to highlight personal characteristics that may not be evident on a resume. It might refer to information you have learned through researching the organization. Always use actual words and phrases directly from the job posting to tip off the reader that you possess the qualifications necessary for the job. Doing so will encourage the reader to examine the attached resume. Because the cover letter is a prelude to the resume, it should not rehash its contents. Do, however, mention that the resume is attached in a body paragraph or the closing.

Closing

The final paragraph of the cover letter must accomplish several things. First, it must ask for an interview. Second, it must provide the best way to contact you for an interview. Avoid sounding too demanding when requesting an interview (*Call me at XXX-XXXX to set up an interview.*) Couch the request in respectful and gracious phrasing. (*I would be grateful for the opportunity to discuss how my skills and experience could benefit Indiana Insurance in an interview. I am best reached after 3 PM at XXX-XXX-XXXX or anytime via e-mail at yourname@aol.com.*)

Cover Letters for Unsolicited Positions

Because up to 80 percent of jobs are not advertised, many job searchers take a proactive approach and send unsolicited job queries to organizations of interest. Such queries require conducting research about the organization: its products, services, corporate philosophy, and news. Learn all you can about a company you wish to work for before sending an unsolicited job inquiry so you can weave the firm's own branding and messaging into your letter.

The elements of unsolicited cover letters are as follows.

Opening

To prevent your letter from being summarily dismissed, grab the reader's attention quickly in your opening statement by including knowledge you've gained about the company's mission, values, or culture. Show how your skills fill a need.

> *The recent news of AdWork's acquisition of Holistic Healing as a client caught my eye because of my knowledge of the complementary medicine field and experience with social media.*

You might also want to use a question to gain interest.

> *Now that Adworks has landed the Holistic Healing account, might you need an experienced social media planner with extensive knowledge of the complementary medicine field?*

Body

The body of an unsolicited job application letter is much like that of the solicited cover letter with the exception of using words and phrases from an ad. Instead, discuss how your skills and experience can benefit the organization or help achieve its goals.

> *My background as the brand manager of a nutriceutical company has given me experience introducing new products to emerging markets.*

Where possible, weave words and phrases the organization uses to describe itself into your letter. For example, if you were writing a letter to Nike, echo words from its mission statement ("to bring inspiration and innovation...") into your letter.

*As a team leader, I **inspired** my group to **innovate** and helped create a successful product line that now comprises 10 percent of company revenues.*

Closing

The closing of the unsolicited and solicited cover letters is the same. Ask for an interview; make sure you refer specifically to an attached resume; avoid vague and clichéd statements such as "Thank you for your time" or "I hope to hear from you soon."

Document Design

If sending the cover letter as an e-mail, make sure your subject line specifically states the job to which you are applying. Begin the e-mail with a formal salutation and follow the document design for e-mails we discussed earlier. Make sure your complete contact information follows your name in the signature block at the end of the e-mail.

If sending a cover letter on paper, print it on the same letterhead you use for your resume. Balance the letter on the page so you don't leave too much white space at the bottom. Remember to physically sign the letter and note *Enclosure* at the end to alert the reader that another piece of paper is part of the package. See Appendix B for a sample cover letter.

Resumes

A resume is a structured summary of your qualifications for a particular position. Many people think resumes need to include their entire work history, listing every job ever held and each commendation earned. This is not the case at all. Resumes must highlight your qualifications as they pertain to the job at hand. As your career advances, your resume will change, too. In other words, you will be rewriting your resume for the rest of your work life!

The most common type of resume is the **chronological resume**, which lists jobs in chronological order from the most current to the oldest. Recruiters are most familiar with this style of resume and prefer it because it quickly illustrates the candidate's education and work background. The **functional resume** includes the same mandatory elements of any resume (heading and education) and many of the same optional sections (objective, and awards, honors, or activities) but highlights skills and abilities instead of job experiences. This style of resume is used for those with gaps in employment or sometimes for new workers who have yet to gather significant on-the-job experience.

The length of resumes is not fixed. Many say a resume should be contained to one typed page; others say it should be as long as it needs to be. Whichever side you choose to believe, remember that experts say that hirers spend no more than five to 10 seconds looking over a resume, so it must be concise and easy to navigate.

Resume sections help your reader move through your information efficiently. Some sections, such as the heading, are mandatory. However, because the resume must introduce you to a potential employer, other sections on your resume may differ from someone else's. The most common sections are shown in Table 8.1 and are further described here.

The **heading** includes the candidate's name and contact information including mailing address, phone, and e-mail address. Some people today opt to omit the address or phone from the heading for privacy concerns. Others may include a website or e-portfolio link.

An **objective** or **career objective** is a statement of a person's desired career trajectory. Experts say it should only be used if it can provide a good argument of how an individual will fit into an organization. This optional category is *not* a statement declaring one's desire for a specific position and should answer certain questions:

- Is the candidate looking for part-time, full-time, or an internship position?
- Which type of position?
- Which industry?
- What qualifications or attributes does the candidate possess that will help the organization meet its goals?

Notice how this example of an objective includes the prior elements without stating a desire for a particular job.

Full-time sales position in retail clothing industry where my education in fashion merchandising and customer service skills will help an organization meet its sales goals.

Table 8.1 Resume sections

Section	Content
Heading	Mandatory. Includes candidate's name, usually in slightly larger font; contact information that may contain address, phone, and e-mail
Objective or career objective	Optional. A sentence describing overall career goal rather than desire for a particular job
Skill summary or summary of qualifications	Optional. Three to eight bulleted points illustrating specific skills either mentioned in job ad or characteristics mentioned in company literature
Education	Mandatory. Name(s) and location of colleges attended including date degree awarded or expected; degree earned (i.e., BA, BS, MA, etc.); major(s) and minor, if applicable; GPA if high or requested; academic honors. Separate subcategory (optional) of Relevant Coursework listing name of course(s) (i.e., Intermediate Accounting, Business Communication, Organic Chemistry, Genetics)
Experience (also referred to as work, professional, or employment experience)	Mandatory in chronological resume; not used in functional resume. List of positions held starting with current job including name of organization, city or state, dates worked, name of position held and followed by list of accomplishments written in specific, terse resume style that omits all articles (*a*, *an*, *the*) and personal pronouns (*I*, *we*)
Skills or capabilities	Optional in chronological resume; mandatory in functional resume. Names skills such as languages spoken, written, and understood, facility with specific computer applications, and personal characteristics illustrating qualities employers would value (i.e., *Excellent collaboration skills*; *Strong verbal and writing skills*). Not used if duplicates information in Skill Summary
Awards, honors, and activities	Optional. Names of awards making sure to explain what name alone may not convey (i.e., Kappa Kappa Kappa Sorority Outstanding Scholar Award; Scholarships; Honors or recognition of service; Certificates; Memberships in professional organizations

A **skill summary** or **summary of qualifications** is an increasingly popular and frequently used section in a resume. It lists, usually in bulleted form, hard skills or personal characteristics the candidate possesses that will immediately catch the reviewer's eye. Pertinent experience, unique skills, accomplishments, or awards can be listed. Often the items included in this category are specific job requirements (such as *Proficiency in Adobe Creative Suite*) taken directly from a job ad.

The **education** category is mandatory for all resumes. However, where it is located changes as you gain more work experience. For students right out of college, the education section may be their most important selling point and therefore follow the heading. However, as people progress through their careers, the education section, though important, is no longer the most important qualification, so it typically is placed lower in the resume.

The education section must include several elements: the name of the institution granting the degree; its location; the date the degree was conferred (or the date the candidate expects to receive the degree); major and minor. GPA is optional and should only be included if it is exceptional (over 3.5).

Many students wonder if they need to include all the colleges they have attended. Again, there is no a rule dictating this choice. If a student attended a community college or studied abroad and took certain pertinent classes or obtained a specific certificate that relates to a job, it would be prudent to include that information in the resume. However, the institution that grants the degree is the one an employer will contact to verify that the degree was indeed conferred.

A subcategory under the education section is **relevant coursework**. For students with little work experience or who have taken courses in which they have practiced tasks specifically mentioned in the job advertisement, this section may be key. For example, if applying for a position that states "Ability to titrate preferred" and the student learned how to titrate in a chemistry class, listing the class and explaining that it required titrating would illustrate that the student possessed that knowledge. When listing courses, never list numbers (Accounting II or Business 145) but the actual name of a course (Intermediate Accounting or Administrative Business Practices).

By far the most important section of a chronological resume is the **experience** category, also referred to as work experience, employment experience, or professional experience. This section lists, in reverse chronological order, jobs held, with the most current job at the beginning. It is not necessary to list every job ever held, just those that relate to the job sought.

Include the following for each job listed:

- Name of employer
- Location
- Dates worked
- Job title (last held or most important)

After that, use bullets (either vertically on separate lines or between phrases within a line) to list relevant job duties, highlighting accomplishments rather than responsibilities. Begin each experience statement with an action verb (*wrote, researched, created, implemented*) in present tense for the current job and past tense for past jobs. Do not use complete sentences; instead, write in truncated, terse, and concise phrases that omit all articles (*a, an, the*). Quantify wherever possible, and weave keywords from the ad into your statements. Avoid personal pronouns (*I, we*) and vary verbs.

Notice how the first statement is vague and wordy.

> *I was responsible for answering the phones in a busy real estate office and making sure the agents turned in various reports*

Rewritten using the truncated resume style, the previous statement would read:

> *Answered 24 phone lines and assured timely return of 16 real estate agents' listings and contact reports*

Use a category named **skills and capabilities** to catalog your specific strengths including languages spoken, written, and understood; mathematics knowledge; computer program use; and expertise with social media, office equipment, or other technology. Also include hard-to-quantify qualities such as the ability to master skills quickly or verbal and written communication skills.

A section naming any **Awards, Honors, and Activities** that pertain to the job at hand or that shows you as a well-rounded individual can be another resume category. For example, if you have achieved a second degree black belt in Tae Kwon Do, you may want to list it as a way to show you have mastered a strenuous mental and physical activity. List scholarships, memberships in professional organizations, or certificates you have been awarded.

What *not* to include in a resume is just as important as what to avoid. *Never* include the following:

- False information
- High school information
- Information listed elsewhere on the resume (don't duplicate information)
- References
- Religious affiliation
- Personal information such as age, race, or gender
- Photograph
- Salary history
- Social security number

Resume Layout and Design

A resume must look as well as it reads. A reader should be able to scan the resume easily to locate sections and read specific items. Employ columns, white space, and clear, legible fonts to make reading your resume less of a chore. Avoid resumes that contain long blocks of dense type. Use graphical devices such as bullets (never use more than one style of bullet), bold face, and italics to highlight consistent categories like dates, locations, and names of organizations. Make sure your margins are at least one inch all around, and if your resume goes onto a second page, provide a second page header with your first initial and last name and page number.

If you want to use color for headings or your name, be conservative. Know that bright colors (fuchsia, magenta, yellow, orange) do not translate well into type. Stick with darker, more conservative colors like green, blue, or maroon. If sending the resume via e-mail, save it as a PDF so your font and color choices are the ones you intend. If printing your resume, use good quality bond paper in ivory, white, or light gray.

Professionalism

Since your resume is your first contact with a potential employer, it is imperative that you show your professionalism. Make sure to proofread carefully; many recruiters and hiring managers say that finding a typo or misspelling on a resume is the single best way to eliminate a candidate. Never lie about an achievement or exaggerate your abilities. Assume a potential employer will check everything you say. (Imagine saying you are fluent in Mandarin when you only know a few words and phrases and having the interviewer begin speaking to you in Mandarin!) Exaggerating a claim is not worth the humiliation of being found out.

See Appendix B for samples of a chronological and a functional resume.

Thank-You Notes

Sending a thank-you note after an interview helps set you apart from other candidates. It is an excellent way to get your name in front of a hirer again and to show your professionalism and writing skills. A thank-you can be sent as a physical letter, either handwritten or typed, or in an e-mail. Never send a thank-you in a text message.

Send a thank-you to each person with whom you spoke at the interview and be sure to get the correct spelling of the name. Thank-you notes need not be long and should never go over one page. It's best to send the thank-you within 24 to 48 hours after the interview.

Use the direct organizational strategy as follows:

- **Direct opening**. Begin with thanking the individual for the opportunity of talking in person. Include a second sentence that mentions an aspect of the interview that stood out to you.
- **Details in body**. Include specifics about something you saw, learned, or omitted in the interview. For example, if you noticed employees collaborating in an open workspace and you work well in such an atmosphere, say so. You may also take this opportunity to bring up something you forgot to say in the interview.
- **Polite close**. Mention that you are excited about the possibility of joining the organization and hope to hear you will be part of the team soon.

See Appendix B for an example of a thank-you letter.

Reference List

A list of people who can vouch about your work-related abilities and your character is an important element of anyone's job search materials. A reference list is generally not included with an initial job query or resume submission. Rather, it is usually provided to a potential employer after an interview or upon request.

Since references speak to your value as an employee, it is best to provide work-related references. If you have not yet been in the workforce, ask professors who can attest to your character or your abilities as a student. Avoid including friends, relatives, or neighbors on a reference list; such people are likely to be ignored by hirers. Once you have had a job, it is wise to ask current supervisors whether they will give you a good reference. After you have determined that someone will offer a positive reference, you may use that individual's name on your reference list. (If you haven't seen or spoken to a reference in a while, notify the individual by e-mail or phone that he or she may be called upon soon to provide a reference for you.)

The reference list should be composed on the same personal letterhead used for the resume. It should include the heading **references** and include the names and contact information for three-to-five professionals. Provide a work phone number instead of a personal cell phone number.

See Appendix B for an example of a Reference List.

LinkedIn

LinkedIn is a social networking site with over 300 million users designed to broaden professionals' networks. Having a presence on LinkedIn is no longer an option for job seekers; it is a requirement. Although the networking site is free, many job seekers choose to pay to upgrade their profiles, which allows them greater access to individuals and to view those looking at their profiles.

When completing a LinkedIn profile, be sure to fill it out thoroughly so it illustrates your career history, education, interests, and other material relevant to the job search. Many suggest having a professional photograph taken to include in the profile.

Perhaps the most important portion of your LinkedIn page is the summary. A LinkedIn summary is a narrative biography that is sometimes called *personal branding.*[2] Limited to 2,000 characters (a letter, punctuation mark, or a space), this imperative piece of your job search materials can not only show off your writing skills but can also reach many potential employers.

As you compose your LinkedIn summary, isolate your purpose and whom you directly want to reach. Use words and phrases likely to speak to that individual. Structure the narrative so it starts with a strong hook and illustrates what makes you stand out. Consider these tips:

- Weave specifics to quantify accomplishments
- Include testimonials to validate your statements[3]
- Compose in short paragraphs
- Use headings to break up longer blocks of text

Many experts suggest including contact information in the summary section, too.

Conclusion

In the competitive arena of hiring today, it is crucial to write clear and effective job search materials. From cover letters that highlight your writing skills and demonstrate your suitability for a job, to a resume that is not only easy to read but also relevant and concise, to a thank-you note or a LinkedIn summary, composing well-written job search materials will be key throughout your professional life.

APPENDIX A

20 Common Writing Errors to Avoid

1. **It's and its**. It's **always** is the contraction for *it is*. *Its* is **never** the possessive of *it*.
   It's hot today.
   The cat chased *its* tail.
2. **Wrong word use**. Using words incorrectly (affect and effect, compliment and complement, they're and their) occurs when words that may sound similar do not mean what the writer thinks. The only fix is to learn the meaning and usage of words.
   Affect = verb. Interest rates *affect* home ownership.
   Effect = noun. The *effect* interest rates have on home ownership is well documented.

   Other potential word use confusions include the following:

   accept/except
   amount/number
   emigrate/immigrate
   lose/loose
   two/too/to
   then/than
   women/woman
3. **Starting sentence with a number**. Never start a sentence with a digit. Spell out the number or rephrase so the number does not begin the sentence.
   Incorrect: 19 candidates applied for the job.
   Correct: *Nineteen* candidates applied for the job. Or, We received 19 applications for the job.

4. **Omitting comma after introductory phrase**. Set off words, phrases, or clauses that introduce a sentence with a comma.

   Incorrect: However the system worked.

   Correct: However, the system worked.

   Incorrect: Because of road closures authorities have had to reroute traffic.

   Correct: Because of the road closures, authorities have had to reroute traffic.

5. **Comma splice**. It is incorrect to use only a comma to separate two independent clauses. Add a coordinate conjunction after the comma.

   Incorrect: The committee decided to table the vote, the members dispersed.

   Correct: The committee decided to table the vote, *and* the members dispersed.

6. **Commas in lists**. Use commas to separate three or more items in a list. Use a comma before *and* and the last item for clarity.

   Incorrect: We have red, black and gray T-shirts.

   Correct: We have red, black, and gray T-shirts.

7. **Ordinals in dates**. Never use ordinals (*st*, *rd*, *th*) when writing a date.

   Incorrect: September 11th, 2001

   Correct: September 11, 2001

8. **Use of capitalization in titles**. Capitalize a title when it precedes a name, but do not capitalize a title when it comes after a name.

   Incorrect: The committee was pleased Drew Pearson was reelected Councilman.

   Correct: The committee was pleased Councilman Drew Pearson was reelected.

9. **Capitalization of directions**. Capitalize geographical areas that are names. Do not capitalize compass directions.

   Incorrect: The warehouse is North of the river.

   Correct: The Southwest boasts many tourist sites.

10. **Confusing lay and lie**. In present tense, lay and lie have different meanings. *Lay* means to place something down. *Lie* means to assume a horizontal position.

    Incorrect: I want to lay down for a nap.

    Correct: I want to *lie* down for a nap.

The past tense for *lay* is *laid*. The past tense for *lie* is *lay*.

Correct: She *laid* down the magazine before checking on the pie.

Correct: After he *lay* down for his nap, the phone awakened him.

11. **Irregardless and regardless**. Although irregardless is a word, it is not considered standard English. Use regardless instead.

    Incorrect: The play will proceed irregardless of bad reviews.

    Correct: The play will proceed *regardless* of bad reviews.

12. **Who and that**. Use who when referring to people; use that when referring to anything else.

    Incorrect: The dog who won in Westminster was from the toy group.

    Correct: The dog *that* won in Westminster was from the toy group.

    Incorrect: The woman that showed the dog also raised it.

    Correct: The woman *who* showed the dog also raised it.

13. **Then and than**. Then refers to time; than shows comparison.

    Incorrect: The group chose red rather then blue flags.

    Correct: Turn left at the first light; *then* proceed three blocks until you reach the dock.

14. **Using you**. Only use *you* when speaking directly to the reader.

    Incorrect: You can only have one child per couple if you live in China.

    Correct: Couples in China can only have one child.

15. **Unnecessary commas**. Do not use a comma before a conjunction to set apart a phrase or clause that share the same verb.

    Incorrect: These rules apply to every home in the city, and to businesses as well.

    Correct: These rules apply to every home in the city and to businesses as well.

16. **Pronoun agreement**. A pronoun must agree with the noun it replaces.

    Incorrect: A candidate will walk among their constituency to poll voters.

    Correct: Candidates will walk among their constituency to poll voters.

17. **Superfluous commas**. Never toss in commas without a reason.

    Incorrect: Fortunately, the men, and the women, of this neighborhood, will likely, participate in the community activities.

    Correct: Fortunately, the men and the women of this neighborhood will likely participate in the community activities.

18. **Tense shift**. Stay in one verb tense in the same sentence.

    Incorrect: When the employee raises the question, the supervisor replied that the decision had already been made.

    Correct: When the employee raised the question, the supervisor replied that the decision had already been made.

19. **Misplaced modifiers**. Place modifiers near the words they modify.

    Incorrect: She gave a brochure to the clients with a key to the lodge.

    Correct: She gave the clients a brochure and a key to the lodge.

20. **Vague pronoun reference**. Make sure pronouns such as *it*, *this*, *these*, and *those* refer to a specific idea or thing.

    Incorrect: The recreation facility provided employees with many exercise options for health and fitness training. It was a popular benefit.

    Correct: The recreation facility provided employees with many exercise options for health and fitness training. The facility was a popular benefit.

APPENDIX B

Document Samples

Chapter 3: Routine and Positive Messages

Direct Request E-mail

Direct Request Response E-mail

Routine Claim

Instruction Memo

Letter

Memo

Routine News E-mail

Thank You

Chapter 4: Persuasive and Bad News Messages

Bad News Letter

Persuasive Request E-mail

Persuasive Memo

Sales Message

Chapter 6: Reports

Trip Report E-mail

Memo Proposal

Letter Report

Chapter 8: Employment Communication

Cover Letter

Chronological Resume

Functional Resume

Thank-You Letter

Reference List

CHAPTER 3

Routine and Positive Messages

Direct Request E-mail

To: Haley Kalekian <kalekian@goodmanners.com>
From: Marsha Gulavsky <marshag@importium.com>
Cc:
Bcc:
Subject: Provide Intercultural Etiquette Workshop in April?

Dear Ms. Kalekian:

Could Good Manners provide a workshop on proper etiquette for dealing with intercultural businesspeople to 50 employees the week of April 4?

I was told of your excellent professional conduct seminars by Lucille Strong at BuyRite Industries, and I am hoping you can tailor your content to meet our needs. We want to prepare our workforce for meeting with potential vendors from Asia, who are visiting our facility April 16. Specifically I would appreciate answers to the questions below.

1. Can you deliver the seminar or workshop at our facilities in Evanston? We have a room with an overhead projector, smart board, and lectern with hookups to most devices.
2. Would our staff have access to the materials you present after the presentation?
3. Could you provide mock situations we could videotape?

Your answers to these questions by February 15 will help me present my recommendations to our management committee.

Sincerely,

Marsha Gulavsky
Training Manager
Importium Industries
1931 Ridge Avenue
Evanston, IL 60201
(847) 903-4886

Direct Request Response E-mail

To: Marsha Gulavsky <marshag@importium.com>
From: Haley Kalekian <kalekian@goodmanners.com>
Cc:
Bcc:
Subject: Your January 21 Request for Intercultural Workshop

Dear Ms. Gulavsky:

Yes, we are available to present a workshop on intercultural business etiquette the week of April 4. Below are the answers to your questions.

1. Our staff regularly travels to clients' places of business, so delivering the workshop in Evanston poses no problem.
2. Part of our service is to leave complete written materials to supplement our presentations. We can prepare materials delivered via PowerPoint or in PDF and can tailor the content to your specific needs.
3. Mock situations are excellent ways to practice certain elements of etiquette and our trainers are schooled in creating specific scenarios that fit your situation.

Intercultural communication can be complex and having your staff attend a workshop would help all involved feel more confident in their ability to successfully communicate with your visitors. Our 15 years of experience in the field and expertise with Asian cultures in particular make me confident that Good Manners would provide Importium Industries with an effective workshop.

I welcome the opportunity to discuss your needs by phone or in person. Please call me at (612) 799-1443 if I can answer any more questions.

Sincerely,

Emma Kalekian
President
Good Manners
112 3rd Street North
Minneapolis, MN 55401
(612) 799-1443
ekalekian@goodmanners.com

Routine Claim

To: Fred Kroll <service@harperhardware.com>
From: Mark Elliot <markelliot@GPM.com>
Subject: Incorrect Order No. MB554-14 Shipped
Cc:
Bcc:

Dear Mr. Kroll:

Please replace Order No. MB-544-14 with the correct chairs I originally ordered.

I placed an order for six conference room chairs, Item 611B. The package arrived with correctly labeled cartons. However, when I opened the boxes, I found the upholstery was patterned instead of solid black.

If you have the black upholstered chairs in stock and can ship them to me immediately, please do so. If not, please refund my credit card charge immediately and provide me with shipping labels to return the incorrect order to Harper Hardware.

Because my firm must use their chairs for an upcoming meeting, I trust that you will let me know within two business days whether you can provide the correct order so that I can explore alternatives if necessary.

Sincerely,

Mark Elliot
Property Manager
Gladd Property Management
429 Forbes Avenue, Suite 75
Pittsburgh, PA 15219
Phone: 412-977-7800

Instruction Memo

MEMO

Date: September 9, 2017
To: Connexion Ltd. Staff
From: Gina Salerno, VP Communications
Subject: Social Media Guidelines

We are all excited to begin our social media campaign and have great confidence your contributions will generate more interaction with our stakeholders.

Please follow these guidelines whenever you contribute to Connexion's social media sites:

1. Identify yourself and your position at Connexion.
2. Write using a natural, respectful tone.
3. Use language your reader will grasp; avoid jargon.
4. Think carefully before posting; think through possible reactions and remember you are a representative of our organization.
5. Revise if you make an error.
6. Contribute thought-provoking, meaningful content.

Following these guidelines will help assure that our social media campaign will bring the kind of results we have outlined. If you have any questions about posting or about content, contact me at Ext. 344.

Letter

2930 Shattuck Avenue
Berkeley, CA 94705
ph: 5 1 0. 9 3 6. 4 9 0 0
fax: 5 1 0. 9 3 6. 4 9 1 0
youradworks.com

February 5, 2016

Mr. Gary Berg, Assistant Director
Holistic Healing
6643 Byland Avenue, Suite 300
Oakland, CA 94602

Dear Mr. Berg:

Thank you for choosing AdWorks to represent Holistic Healing in its marketing and advertising efforts. We are confident our plans will effectively boost Holistic Healing's visibility in the booming alternative medicine arena.

Enclosed are two copies of the marketing representation agreement, which include the revised advertising and social media plan schedules we discussed on the phone today. Please sign both copies of the agreement and return them, along with the retainer mentioned in Section II, Point A, no later than February 10 so we can meet the aggressive deadlines we have set. We will return an executed copy to you as soon as we receive your signed agreements.

We look forward to working closely with you and the rest of the Holistic Healing team over the next year.

Sincerely,

Rich Gold

Richard Gold, President
AdWorks

Memo

Date: February 5, 2016
To: Manny Doran, Media Services Manager
Elizabeth Dowley, Creative Director
From: Rich Gold, President
Subject: Holistic Healing Account and Scheduling

Now that we have landed the Holistic Healing account, we need to focus our energies on meeting the aggressive deadlines set in the contract. Below are the two main areas on which we should concentrate.

Relationship Building
To foster goodwill and build strong working relationships, we should set up a series of meetings and lunches in which our key people meet with the Holistic Healing team. Be sure your staff goes into these meetings fully armed with research and knowledge about this market so when they spend time at the site, they can better absorb details. This is a new arena for us, and we need to get up to speed quickly.

Branding/Creative
By March, we should be working on creative approaches to bring to the client by the end of the month. That will include recommendations for:

- Print/online media with CPM estimates
- Social media strategy: Blog, Facebook, Instagram, etc.
- Branding
- Storyboards/print ad/online ads

Please send me a progress report detailing your plans to meet these goals by noon on Thursday, February 11. This will be a busy few months, but I'm certain your teams are up to the task.

Routine News E-mail

New Parking Policy Effective June 1

Send | Chat | Attach | Address | Fonts | Colors | Save As Draft | Photo Browser | Show Stationery

To: K&P Staff

Cc:

Bcc:

Subject: New Parking Policy Effective June 1

From: Isobel Sanchez <i.sanchex@k&p.com>

Dear K&P Colleagues:

A new policy giving preferred parking to carpools will take effect on Monday, June 1, 2016.

The policy comes from the recommendations of the ad hoc committee on sustainability as a way to improve our "green profile" while also addressing the current issue of overcrowding in our parking lot.

To be eligible for these spots, carpools must be comprised of at least three employees who register their carpools with the Human Relations Department. Carpoolers will receive a removable sticker to be placed on the windshield of the driver's vehicle and will park directly next to the building's back exit.

The desirable spots will go to the first 15 carpools that register with HR before Thursday, May 25. Please contact me with any questions you have about the policy.

Sincerely,

Izzy

Isobel Sanchez, Administrative Liaison
Human Relations
i.sanchez@k&p.com I (206)650-4055 ext. 29

Thank You

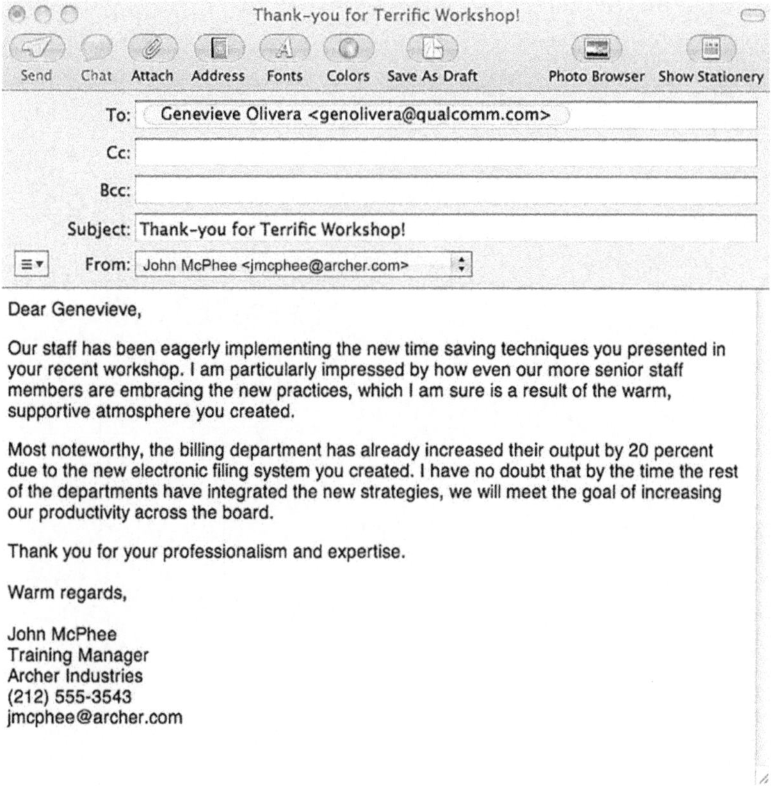

Thank-you for Terrific Workshop!

Send Chat Attach Address Fonts Colors Save As Draft Photo Browser Show Stationery

To: Genevieve Olivera <genolivera@qualcomm.com>

Cc:

Bcc:

Subject: Thank-you for Terrific Workshop!

From: John McPhee <jmcphee@archer.com>

Dear Genevieve,

Our staff has been eagerly implementing the new time saving techniques you presented in your recent workshop. I am particularly impressed by how even our more senior staff members are embracing the new practices, which I am sure is a result of the warm, supportive atmosphere you created.

Most noteworthy, the billing department has already increased their output by 20 percent due to the new electronic filing system you created. I have no doubt that by the time the rest of the departments have integrated the new strategies, we will meet the goal of increasing our productivity across the board.

Thank you for your professionalism and expertise.

Warm regards,

John McPhee
Training Manager
Archer Industries
(212) 555-3543
jmcphee@archer.com

CHAPTER 4

Persuasive and Bad News Messages

Bad News Letter

HAPPY VALLEY HISTORICAL SOCIETY

52 HILLVIEW DRIVE **HAPPY VALLEY, OR 97015**
(503) 356-9954 **WWW.HVHISTORY.COM**

February 5, 2016

Mrs. Margaret Sangford
11 Park Drive
Happy Valley, OR 97015

Dear Mrs. Sangford:

Thank you for your well researched proposal to include Mayweather House in this year's *Giving Back*® volunteer day. Mayweather House's distinctive architectural style and garden is indeed one that merits preservation for future generations.

As you may be aware, our primary goal is to improve homes in our town's most neglected areas. We gave close consideration to the 22 submissions we received and were able to include the 10 homes in the most dire condition for this year's rehabilitation efforts. While Mayweather House was not one of the selected properties, we encourage you to apply again next year.

We are grateful that citizens like you take the effort to support our ongoing efforts to improve our town and share your commitment to bring Happy Valley's architectural gems back to their original glory.

Sincerely,

Annabel McElmurray
Annabel McElmurray
President

Persuasive Request E-mail

To: Marian Mintner <mminter@temphelp4you.com>
From: Juanita Eastman <jleastman@aol.com>
Subject: Invitation to Speak to UCLA Bruin Business Students
Cc:
Bcc:

Dear Ms. Mintner:

As a former Bruin whose thriving business is legendary among current UCLA business students, your success story would be an inspiration to members of the Accounting Association.

Because of our club's focus on business and your success as an entrepreneur, you would be the perfect speaker to get our club off to a great start this year. Your expertise as well as your history with our campus will make your talk a big draw for our members. With their business and accounting backgrounds, some students in our club may even be potential employees at TempHelp4You.

I hope you'll accept my invitation to be the keynote speaker at the Business and Accounting Association's annual kick-off meeting. The meeting will be held on Wednesday, September 10, 2016, from noon until 1:30 p.m. in Room 101 of the Anderson School of Management Building. We would like you to speak for about 30 minutes and then take questions from the audience. On the day of the event, we are happy to provide you with lunch and a complimentary parking permit, which you would pick up at the information kiosk at the main entrance to campus.

Please let me know if you can speak at our meeting by August 20 so I can make the appropriate arrangements. You can phone me at (310) 544-2181 or e-mail me at jleastman@aol.com if you have any questions. I hope to see you in September!

Sincerely,

Juanita Eastman
Public Relations Director
UCLA Accounting Association

Persuasive Memo

Mission Radiology

MEMO

DATE: March 3, 2016
TO: Staff
FROM: Dan Marciano, President
SUBJ: Increase Wellness + Decrease Insurance Costs = Win,Win!

Thanks to all our hardworking staff who have helped Mission Radiology once again be named the best provider of imaging services in Santa Barbara!

As much as we value providing compassionate care and unparalleled service to our patients, we are likewise committed to helping our staff improve and maintain their own health. We know dealing with sick and worried patients every day can be stressful, which is why we are pleased to announce our new Wellness Program.

This optional program is designed to help you lower stress, increase stamina, and improve your overall health and fitness. You'll be able to choose from a variety of activities such as biometric screenings, one-on-one health coaching, smoking cessation clinics, and discounts at local gyms.

Mission Radiology is so enthusiastic about our Wellness Program that we will reduce your health insurance premium by $100 each month. All you have to do is sign up, set up your own goals, and meet them within a designated time frame.

Take advantage now by joining us at the informational meeting on Wednesday, October 14, in the patient waiting room at 6:00 p.m. Everyone attending will receive a free 10-minute neck massage, so don't miss out!

Sales Message

To: <clientname@yahoo.com>
From: DeeDee's Delights <www.deedeesdelectables.com>
Subject: Enjoy 15% Off DeeDee's Delectable Sugar-Free Desserts
Cc:
Bcc:

Dear Dessert Lover,

So you're diabetic ... you can still have dessert!

DeeDee's Delectable sugar-free desserts are made from the purest ingredients, contain no sugar, and are low in carbs. From chocolate mousse to raspberry cheesecake, our mouth-watering selections will satisfy your craving for delicious sweets.

Right now, we're offering new customers an added incentive to try our award-winning goodies. Visit DeeDee's Delectables and enjoy 15% off your first order. But order today ... offer ends April 2. Call 1(800) DESSERT or order online at www.deedeesdelectables.com.

Tastefully,

The DeeDee Team

CHAPTER 6

Reports

Trip Report E-mail

To:	Elvin Lucas
From:	Avi Ben Shimon
Subject:	Trip Report, CES 2016
Cc:	
Bcc:	
Date:	January 12, 2016

Dear Elvin,

The following report describes my recent trip to the annual Computer Electronics Show in Las Vegas from January 6 to 9. I will provide key contacts in the sectors of the show we agreed to focus on.

Cyber Security. GoldKey, out of Missouri, features a dual-factor authentication device that has secure e-mail, encrypted Cloud storage, and fully supporting gold pay. My contact there was Dumont Price. Our initial meeting was very productive, and I will follow up with him regularly.

Personal Privacy. iWallet, in San Diego, produces a high-tech security solution to protect passports and other valuables. I met with Mercedes Previn, and we have a video chat planned for later this week to discuss providing them with our fingerprint capture technology. I will update you following our chat.

Also from this marketplace, I made a great connection with Lou Martine at Private Internet Access, headquartered in Los Angeles. Lou and I spent several hours discussing personal privacy technology, and I feel optimistic about our ability to supply them with our products. I will remain in contact.

This year's convention was definitely productive. I'll keep you posted about progress on the connections I made there.

Memo Proposal

EC Consultants

DATE: July 16, 2016
TO: Hae Ryu, Senior Vice President and Director of Marketing
FROM: Elizabeth Condren
RE: Proposal for American Business Bank & Trust Wealth Management Project

Thank you for the opportunity to propose a plan to implement the Wealth Management document revision project we have discussed. This proposal includes a description of proposed services, schedule, and fee structure.

Situation Analysis

American Business Bank & Trust Wealth Management division stands poised to take advantage of the current market in which the banking upheaval has led to weak performance among some local competitors. To attract a greater market share of those with portfolios of over $500,000, ABB&T seeks to refine its communications with current and potential clients.

In addition, the bank—perhaps at a later date—wishes to streamline the internal written communication approval process by providing key personnel with predetermined words and phrases that can be plugged into working templates of standardized documents. Attending to Wealth Management's documents marks the first step in this process.

Statement of Purpose

This proposal defines the scope of services and cost to refine documents originating from ABB&T Wealth Management to help secure greater market share.

Goals and Objectives Timetable

The following table provides a breakdown of individual tasks and a timetable of their duration. This schedule is obviously dependent upon availability of involved parties.

Hae Ryu Page 2 July 16, 2016

Goal/ Objective/Task	Description	Those Involved	Estimated Duration
Analyze current documents	Analyze ABB&T sample written documents to isolate communication issues and problems	Corporate Communication and Marketing personnel and EC consultant	½ to 1 day
Create templates for revised documents	Develop templates with input and approval from ABB&T marketing staff	EC consultant	~3 days
Create consistent document design	Provide recommendations for graphic improvements of presentation materials, working with ABB&T marketing staff	Corporate Communication and Marketing personnel and EC consultant	~3 days
Meet with key players for template user instruction	Provide one-on-one (or group) workshops to enhance understanding of both written and graphical elements in newly developed ABB&T documents	Various ABB&T Staff and EC consultant	½ to 1 day

Budget

EC Consultants' fee to implement the above plan of action will be $8,500. This will include delivery of final camera-ready art. All other materials, facilities, and resources will be provided by ABB&T.

Conclusion

My experience in the banking industry as well as my background as a professional writer and writing professor provide a targeted skill set that will allow ABB&T to attain the stated goals and objectives. I look forward to working with the bank's management to start work on this project and eagerly await your approval. With your approval, I am available to begin implementation of the project as early as September 1.

Letter Report

WaterWise Landscape Services

P.O. Box 22460 (858-332-4112)
San Diego, CA www.waterwise.com

November 17, 2016

Richard San Fermo
Bernardo Heights Condominium Association
6100 La Flecha Avenue
Rancho Santa Fe, CA 92091

Dear Mr. San Fermo:
Thank you for your inquiry about drought-resistant landscaping for your condominium complex. Below are the services we offer that can help your association meet county-mandated water saving practices.

Lawn Conversion
Redesign underutilized lawns into a seating area with decomposed granite and San Diego native shrubs, fruit trees, and small kitchen gardens. We use the innovative technique of sheet mulching, a simple method used to enrich the soil in planting areas, establish a new landscape or garden area, or remove a lawn without herbicides.

Ground Cover
Drought tolerant ground covers can add visual interest to a landscape. Some varieties grow in a low mound while others are higher. Ground covers have the added benefit of helping avoid erosion.

Drought Tolerant Landscape
A mixture of hardscaping with drought tolerant native plants will reduce water use. During extreme droughts, these plants will exist primarily on natural rainfall.

R. San Fermo Page 2 November 17, 2015

Trees

Stone fruit trees such as peach, apricot, and some cherries as well as several other varieties—almond and pistachio in particular—do well in hot climates. Scattering trees among shrubs and groundcover is a good way to add shade and beauty.

Drip Irrigation

Changing water wasting, above ground sprinklers with drip irrigation can save hundreds of gallons of water each month. Drip irrigation delivers water to individual plant roots through an underground network of tubes or pipes.

We look forward to meeting with you to assess your landscaping needs. Please call us at (858) 332-4112 for a free consultation.

Sincerely,

Rob Guillermo

Rob Guillermo
President

CHAPTER 8

Employment Communication

Cover Letter

To: John Grigson <jgrigson@altagraphics.com>
From: Gary Fried <G.Fried@gmail.com>
Subject: Graphic Artist Position Posted
Date: January 7, 2015
cc:
Bcc:

Dear Mr. Grigson,

The Graphic Artist job you posted today on Craigslist immediately caught my eye. My skills and experience as a first rate designer—especially with print, advertising, and web graphics—combined with my abilities as a creative copywriter would make me an invaluable asset to your team.

With my current freelance customers and in my previous positions as the primary design resource within a company, I have served as an integral member of tight-knit groups. I thrive in an atmosphere where I am called upon to produce effective branding, advertising, and collateral materials for print, trade shows, and web formats. I am excited about the prospect of joining a firm such as MarkeTrends because of its reputation as an innovative and trend-setting organization, which meshes with my approach to design.

After you've had a chance to examine the attached visual and traditional resumes, I'd like the opportunity to meet with you in person to show you how my positive attitude can help MarkeTrends attain its goals. I am available to talk at (XXX-XXX-XXXX) or via e-mail at (G.Fried@gmail.com).

Sincerely,

Gary Fried
(XXX-XXX-XXXX)
G.Fried@gmail.com
www.linkedin.com/profile

Chronological Resume

41 Holly Glen Lane,
Berkeley Heights, NJ 07922
(201) 688-7465

Jake Cohen jakecohen234@gmail.com

Skills Summary

- Proficient in Photoshop, Illustrator, InDesign, Acrobat
- Knowledgeable in Quark, Final Cut Pro, Flash, DreamWeaver, Microsoft Office
- Creative problem solver and team player
- Strong verbal and written communication skills

Professional Experience

Creative Concepts, Inc. Hoboken, NJ
Art Director 2010–present

- Provided creative direction and design of branding, packaging, advertising, product catalogs, support/marketing materials, and website presence for mass-market consumer goods manufacturer
- Created and oversaw graphic design and engineering for packaging, POP displays, sales brochures and support materials, print and web ads, and promotions, resulting in 23% growth in sales with retailers including Walmart, Toys "R" Us, Barnes & Noble, Target, and Amazon

Miracle Marketing Albany, NY
Designer 2006–2010

- Collaborated with photographers, copywriters, illustrators, and art licensors to create advertising campaigns resulting in 25% sales increase for clients
- Conceptualized and executed presentations to gain new business
- Worked under tight timeframes to meet aggressive deadlines

Jake Cohen Designs Albany, NY
Owner/Designer 2004–2006

- Founded/ran freelance design firm to create effective print/web ads, logos, packaging, winning "Best Designer" in *AlbanyWeekly* competition

Education

Rochester Institute of Technology Rochester, NY
BFA Graphic Design, High Honors May, 2004

Memberships

American Institute of Graphic Artists
Member 2002–present

Functional Resume

Shenyang Wu
(925) 200-4659
Shenwu@aol.com

P.O. Box 24456
Oakland, CA 94601

Objective Position in informational technology where my knowledge of computer applications and proven communication skills can assist an organization meet its goals

Computer Skills

- Proficient in Microsoft Office (all versions)
- Expertise with Adobe CS
- Proficient in social media networking
- Capable in HTML coding
- Comfortable with Mac and PC platforms

Communication Skills

- Wrote business plan, winning campus-wide entrepreneurial start-up award of $5,000
- Spoke before angel investors to presenting idea for start-up business that secured $10,000

Organizational Skills

- Multitasked two part-time jobs while taking full load of university courses
- Assisted in restructuring of fundraising database resulting in 20% increased donations

Management Skills

- Helped complete tight deadlines in semester-long projects
- Motivated interns at start-up dotcom, resulting in promotion within 3 months

Education BS, May 2014, University of British Columbia, 2013

Major: Computer Science
Minor: Technology Management
GPA: 3.7

Employment *Virtual Realities*, Vancouver, Canada, 2013–2014
CanPro.com, San Francisco, CA 2014

Thank-You Letter

Martina Sanchez
2837 Dupont Avenue #34
Minneapolis, MN 55408
(612) 521-7790
msanchez@gmail.com

May 13, 2016

Mr. Robert Wickham, Claims Manager
Grove Insurance
219 2nd Street North
Minneapolis, MN 55403

Dear Mr. Wickham:

Thank you for the opportunity to discuss Grove Insurance's business and the Adjuster position in the Claims Department today.

I was particularly impressed to witness the intake telephone call and could see that Grove is committed to providing its customers with excellent service. As we discussed, my past position as a customer service representative in a busy retail store has provided me with the skill and experience to handle such situations with finesse.

As I left the interview, I was reminded of a time that illustrated my ability to multitask under a tight deadline. As part of a team writing a research report for a class project, I stepped in to cover the absence of several members of the group who became ill three days before the project was due. While completing my section, I also edited and proofread my teammates' sections and created the PowerPoint for the oral presentation. This was particularly challenging because I was simultaneously working at a part-time job. I am pleased to say we turned the project in on time and earned an "A."

I am eager to become part of such an established and respected company and hope to hear from you soon.

Sincerely,
Martina Sanchez

Reference List

Marjorie McMannis
P.O. Box 3376 Encino, CA 91436
mmcmannis@gmail.com
(818) 555-4441

Ms. Jessica Harkness
Public Outreach Manager
Western Bank
11567 Grand Street
Los Angeles, CA 90012
(213) 898-0900 ext. 24
jharkness@western.com

Mr. David Eastman
Intern Supervisor
Kohl & Associates
18443 Ventura Boulevard Suite 206
Tarzana, CA 91356
(818) 988-5771
david.eastman@kohl.com

Prof. Ellen Scribner
UCLA English Department
149 Humanities Building
Box 951530
Los Angeles - CA 90095 - 1530
(310) 336-7687

Notes

Chapter 2

1 Nielsen (1996).

Chapter 3

1 Feintzeig (2014).
2 Alred, Brusaw, and Oliu (2014), p. 47.
3 Guffey and Loewy (2015), p. 207.
4 Martin (2014).
5 Alred, Brusaw, and Oliu (2014), p. 49.
6 Guffey and Loewy (2013), p. 108.
7 "Nine Steps to More Effective Business Emails" (2013).
8 "Nine Steps to More Effective Business Emails" (2013).
9 Covey (2012), p. 145.

Chapter 4

1 Guffey and Loewy (2015), p. 158.
2 Marsh, Guth, and Short (2012), p. 32.

Chapter 5

1 Intel.com (2015).
2 Smith (2013).
3 Maltby (2013).
4 Community Health Maps.com (2014).
5 Community Health Maps.com (2014).
6 Maltby and Ovide (2013).
7 Bourque (2012).

Chapter 6

1 McMahon (2014).
2 Covey (2012), p. 270.
3 Newman (2015), p. 335.

Chapter 7

1 Duarte (2008), p. 5.
2 Dumont (2015).
3 Latta (2014).
4 Reynolds (2014).
5 Kawasaki (2005).
6 Reynolds (2014).
7 Duarte (2010).
8 Duarte (2008).
9 Godin (2001).
10 Reynolds (2008).
11 Reynolds (2011).

Chapter 8

1 Doyle (2015).
2 Arruna (2014).
3 Arruna (2014).

References

Alred, G.J., C.T. Brusaw, and W. Oliu. 2014. *The Business Writer's Companion.* 7th ed. Boston, MA: Bedford St. Martin's.

Arruna, W. September 7, 2014. "Three Steps to Writing the Perfect Linked In Summary." Forbes.com. http://www.forbes.com/sites/williamarruda/2014/09/07/three-steps-to-writing-the-perfect-linkedin-summary/ (accessed January 19, 2015).

Bourque, A. 2012. "Intel's Social "Status Update": Make Conversations, Not Ads." Technorati.com. http://technorati.com/intels-social-status-update-make-conversations-not-ads-2/ (accessed January 19, 2015).

Community Health Maps 2014. "How Accurate Is the GPS on My Smartphone? (Part I)." http://communityhealthmaps.nlm.nih.gov/2014/06/30/how-accurate-is-the-gps-on-my-smartphone/(accessed January 19, 2015).

Covey, S. 2012. *Style Guide for Business and Technical Communication.* 5th ed. Upper Saddle River, NJ: FT Press.

Doyle, A. 2015. "How Often Do People Change Jobs?" Jobsearch.about.com. http://jobsearch.about.com/od/employmentinformation/f/change-jobs.htm (accessed January 19, 2015).

Duarte, N. 2008. *Slide:ology: The Art and Science of Creating Great Presentations.* Sebastapol, CA: O'Reilly Media.

Duarte, N. 2010. *Resonate: Present Visual Stories That Transform Audiences.* Hoboken, NJ: John Wiley & Sons.

Dumont, J. 2015. "Effective Oral Presentations." Treesmapsandtheorems.com. http://www.treesmapsandtheorems.com/pdfs/TM&Th-3.0-summary.pdf (accessed January 19, 2015).

Feintzeig, R. 2014. "A Company Without Email? Not So Fast." Wsj.com, June 17. http://online.wsj.com/news/article_email/a-company-without-email-not-so-fast-1403048134-lMyQjAxMTA0MDEwODExNDgyWj?mod=djem_jiewr_IT_domainid

Godin, S. 2001. "Really Bad PowerPoint." Sethgodin.com. http://www.sethgodin.com/freeprize/reallybad-1.pdf (accessed January 19, 2015).

Guffey, M., and D. Loewy. 2013. *Essentials of Business Communication.* 9th ed. Mason, OH: South-Western Cengage Learning.

Guffey, M., and D. Loewy. 2015. *Business Communication: Process and Product.* 8th ed. Stamford, CT: Cengage Learning.

Intel.com. 2015. "Intel Social Media Guidelines." http://www.intel.com/content/www/us/en/legal/intel-social-media-guidelines.html (accessed January 19, 2015).

Kawasaki, G. 2005. "The 10/20/30 Rule of PowerPoint." *Guykawasaki* (blog), December 30. http://blog.guykawasaki.com/2005/12/the_102030_rule.html (accessed January 19, 2015).

Latta, J. July 16, 2014. "3 is a Magic Number—for Proposals and Presentations." Multibriefs.com. http://exclusive.multibriefs.com/content/3-is-a-magic-number-for-proposals-and-presentations (accessed January 19, 2015).

Maltby, E. January 31, 2013. "Some Social-Media Tips for Business Owners." Wsj.com. http://live.wsj.com/video/social-media-tips-for-small-businesses/1688579B-EA7C-4C6A-B16B-4369A053F50A.html?KEYWORDS=emily+maltby#!1688579B-EA7C-4C6A-B16B-4369A053F50A (accessed January 19, 2015).

Maltby, E., and S. Ovide. 2013. "Small Firms Say LinkedIn Works, Twitter Doesn't." *The Wall Street Journal*, January 31, p. B8.

Marsh, C., D. Guth, and B. Short. 2012. *Strategic Writing: Multimedia Writing for Public Relations, Advertising and More.* 3rd ed. Upper Saddle River, NJ: Pearson Education.

Martin, E. 2014. "The 12 Most Common Email Mistakes Professionals Make." BusinessInsider.com, July 10. http://www.businessinsider.com/common-email-mistakes-professionals-make-2014-7 (accessed January 19, 2015).

McMahon, G. May 28, 2014. "Stop Decking Around; 7 Ways to Use PowerPoint." Makeapowerfulpoint.com. http://makeapowerfulpoint.com/2014/05/28/stop-decking-around-7-ways-use-powerpoint/ (accessed January 10, 2015).

Newman, A. 2015. *Business Communication: In Person, In Print, Online.* 9th ed. Stamford, CT: Cengage Learning.

Nielsen, J. February 1, 1996. "In Defense of Print." Nielsonnormangroup.com. http://www.nngroup.com/articles/in-defense-of-print/ (accessed January 19, 2015).

"Nine Steps to More Effective Business Emails." October 15, 2013. A Blog for the Comma Man. http://freestyle-blog.com/2013/10/15/nine-steps-to-more-effective-business-emails/ (accessed January 19, 2015).

Reynolds, G. 2008. *Presentation Zen: Simple Ideas on Presentation Design and Delivery.* Berkeley, CA: New Riders.

Reynolds, G. 2011. *The Naked Presenter: Delivering Powerful Presentations With or Without Slides.* Berkeley, CA: New Riders.

Reynolds, G. 2014. Presentation Tips. Garreynolds.com. http://www.garrreynolds.com/preso-tips (accessed January 19, 2015).

Smith, K. 2013. "I Just Tried on Google Glass, and This Is What It Was Like." BusinessInsider.com, March 12. http://www.businessinsider.com/normal-person-trying-on-google-glass-2013-3#ixzz2NNWC4OaJ

Index

OTHER TITLES IN THE CORPORATE COMMUNICATION COLLECTION

Debbie DuFrene, Stephen F. Austin State University, Editor

- *Corporate Communication: Tactical Guidelines for Strategic Practice* by Michael Goodman and Peter B. Hirsch
- *Communication Strategies for Today's Managerial Leader* by Deborah Roebuck
- *Communication in Responsible Business: Strategies, Concepts, and Cases* by Roger N. Conaway and Oliver Laasch
- *Web Content: A Writer's Guide* by Janet Mizrahi
- *Intercultural Communication for Managers* by Michael B. Goodman
- *Today's Business Communication: A How-To Guide for the Modern Professional* by Jason L. Snyder and Robert Forbus
- *Fundamentals of Writing for Marketing and Public Relations: A Step-by-Step Guide for Quick and Effective Results* by Janet Mizrahi
- *Managerial Communication: Evaluating the Right Dose* by J. David Johnson
- *Leadership Talk: A Discourse Approach to Leader Emergence* by Robyn Walker and Jolanta Aritz
- *Communication Beyond Boundaries* by Payal Mehra
- *Managerial Communication* by Reginald L. Bell and Jeanette S. Martin
- *Managerial Communication: Evaluating the Right Dose* by J. David Johnson
- *Persuasive Business Presentations: Using the Problem-Solution Method to Influence Decision Makers to Take Action* by Gary May
- *SPeak Performance: Using the Power of Metaphors to Communicate Vision, Motivate People, and Lead Your Organization to Success* by Jim Walz
- *Leadership Talk: A Discourse Approach to Leader Emergence* by Robyn Walker and Jolanta Aritz

CPSIA information can be obtained
at www.ICGtesting.com
Printed in the USA
BVHW041529040422
633306BV00008B/157

9 781631 572326